KEYS TO CONSERVATIVE INVESTMENTS

INVESTMENTS

Second Edition

KEYS TO CONSERVATIVE INVESTMENTS

Second Edition

Nicholas G. Apostolou, DBA, CPA

U.J. LeGrange Professor of Accounting
Louisiana State University

BARRON'S

All inquiries should be addressed to:
Barron's Educational Series, Inc.
250 Wireless Boulevard
Hauppauge, NY 11788

Library of Congress Catalog Card Number 95-42798

International Standard Book Number 0-8120-9006-3

Library of Congress Cataloging-in-Publication Data
Apostolou, Nicholas G.
        Keys to conservative investments / Nicholas G. Apostolou. —
2nd ed.
        p.   cm. — (Barron's business keys)
        Includes index.
        ISBN 0-8120-9006-3
        1. Investments. I. Title. II. Series.
HG4521.A63   1996
332.6—dc20   95-42798
                                            CIP

PRINTED IN THE UNITED STATES OF AMERICA

6789   9770   98765432

CONTENTS

1

INTRODUCTION

This book is intended to help you find safe, secure investments for which your return will exceed that of a passbook savings account. Most people don't save enough and don't invest properly. Investing profitably is not complicated. To be a successful investor, you don't have to pick the right individual stocks or call market turns. In addition, you don't have to assume substantial risk. You can earn solid returns with no loss of sleep.

To accumulate substantial savings, you have to start now. Even small amounts can grow to substantial sums if invested wisely. For example, if you invest $1,000 a year at 8 percent compounded annually, at the end of ten years you would have $14,487. At the end of twenty years, your savings would reach $45,762. The sooner you invest, the fatter your retirement nest egg will become.

Building an investment portfolio begins with self-assessment. You have to determine your objectives or goals and what you are willing and able to do to meet your goals before you can start an investment plan. Once you have established your financial goals, consider what resources you have available, what level of risk you are willing to assume, and what strategies you wish to pursue.

Before making specific investments, you need to have an amount at least equal to your salary for three months in bank savings or a money market mutual fund. In addition, make certain you have adequate medical and life insurance. Once these needs have been met, you are ready to invest.

Many small investors assume their alternatives are limited. This book shows otherwise. It describes different investments, the risks you assume, and the returns you can expect. The investment vehicles discussed are the ones appropriate for investors who are hesitant to assume substantial risk. Derivative instruments such as options and futures are not in this book. These vehicles are not appropriate for the small investor.

This book strongly advocates well-managed, no-load mutual funds as a way to build your portfolio. More than 40 million people own 7,000 mutual funds of which the total assets exceed $3 trillion. Pooling is the principal advantage of mutual fund investing. By pooling the resources of thousands of investors, mutual funds give you access to the knowledge of the nation's top money managers, wide diversification of ownership in the securities market, and a variety of services otherwise only available to institutions and wealthy individuals. For as little as $250, you can join the pros instead of trying to beat them.

One rule that will be repeatedly stressed is the importance of diversification. Diversification involves the spreading of risk by putting your savings in several categories of investments such as stocks, bonds, and money market instruments. You can further diversify by buying stocks in different industries and by choosing different types of stock such as growth, small company, international, etc. Diversification can substantially cut risk with small reductions in return. The old adage of never putting all your eggs in one basket applies particularly to investing. Diversification insures that no single stock or bond will drop precipitously and endanger the security of your portfolio.

Finally, a main theme of this book is the importance of participating in the stock market. Fixed-income investments such as bonds and certificates of deposit (CDs) are appropriate for a portion of your portfolio, but you should remember that historically the real return on these investments after allowing for inflation and taxes is near zero. To increase your real wealth, you should put the bulk of your long-term money into stock-owning mutual funds. Forget about the ups and downs of the stock market. In the long run, the stock market will reflect the earnings generated by corporations which should at least double over the next decade.

2

ASSET ALLOCATION

Before beginning an investment program, every investor should map out his or her own financial profile. A wise investor must begin with self analysis. Certain questions need to be answered: What are my objectives and goals? What is my net worth? How much risk am I willing to assume?

Perhaps the first step in any investment program is to identify your goals and objectives. These goals need to be written down and referred to when setting up your investment program. Your goals should be divided into intermediate or near-term (within the next several years) and long-range goals.

Before making any investment, you must know your net worth. This process enables you to match your investment to your resources and to accomplish your financial goals. The calculation is simple. Calculate the current value of everything you own and add up the numbers; the total is your assets. Subtract from your total assets the value of everything you owe (your liabilities). The difference between your total assets and your total liabilities is your net worth.

The concept of risk is often overlooked when the returns from various investments are cited. As a general rule, the more risk you assume, the higher the potential return is. Your net worth and your potential income are factors in dictating the amount of risk you can assume. Of further importance is the psychological aspect of assuming risk. No investment should be entered into if it causes anxiety and loss of sleep.

In addition, you should examine the adequacy of your life insurance and disability coverage and establish an emergency fund. An emergency fund consists of bank savings or money market funds that are available to meet unexpected needs. An investor should plan on the possibility of paying unexpected expenses without having to liquidate long-term investments. An amount equal to three months of your salary should be sufficient.

In his book, *Asset Allocation: Balancing Financial Risk* (Dow Jones-Irwin), Roger Gibson says, "Successful investing has very little to do with complicated tasks like picking the right individual stocks or calling market turns." Gibson contends that the most important decision in investing is how you divide your money between stocks, bonds, and cash. For support he cites a study in the July—August 1986 issue of Financial *Analysts Journal* that evaluated the ten-year performance of 91 pension funds. The study concluded that 94 percent of the funds' returns were due to the way investments were allocated, while only 6 percent resulted from market timing and from specific picks within each asset group.

In the past, common stocks have been the best long-term investment. However, common stocks entail considerable risk. They can go down or up substantially. Investors should not be misled by the booming stock market of the 1980–1995 period when stocks (measured by Standard & Poor's 500 Index) went up an average of 15 percent a year. This period was one of the great bull markets in stock market history. It is not likely to be repeated over the next 15 years.

Investors should remember one of Wall Street's oldest rules: diversification reduces risk. Well-diversified portfolios containing stocks, bonds, cash, or their mutual fund counterparts, can reduce volatility in investment returns. Even better, volatility can be reduced with only a small reduction in potential return. The best investment over the period from 1985 to 1994 was common stock, which returned an average of 14.40 percent as measured by Standard & Poor's 500 Index. Meanwhile, treasury bonds returned 11.06 percent over the same period. However, for the investor with a diversified portfolio, risk was reduced with only a minor sacrifice in return. A portfolio of 60 percent stocks and 40 percent treasury bonds would have returned about 13 percent over the period.

3

RISK AND RETURN

As previously mentioned, common stocks have on average proven to be excellent investments. With an average return of more than 10 percent, common stocks have substantially outperformed corporate bonds and government securities. However, investors have to remember the risks associated with these generous returns. In 1973–74, the Dow Jones Industrial Average dropped by almost half from 1051.70 to 577.60. On October 19, 1987, the stock market collapsed, free falling 508 points. The drop in the Dow on October 19, 1987 was 22.6 percent, even greater than the crash of October 29, 1929 when the Dow closed lower by 12.8 percent. The stock market will not climb upward in a smooth, predictable pattern. Periodically, there will be steep losses jarring the confidence of investors. Investors should not panic when these drops occur but look at them as potential opportunities.

Any investment involves a trade-off between risk and reward. The higher the reward, the greater the risks and uncertainties are likely to be. It's not informative to know that a stock picker beat the market if you don't know the risk that was assumed. Wise investors examine a strategy's riskiness in addition to its performance.

Although common stock has certainly proved to be rewarding for investors, risks and uncertainties are associated with their purchase. Your investment will fluctuate in price over a substantial range if held for several years. Don't expect to buy a stock at its low price for the year. Individual investors should be looking at a time horizon of three to five years. Ultimately, it will be the company's success in generating future earnings that will most influence the price of its stock. However, over any given period stock prices will fluctuate widely in response to company news, changes in industry conditions, economic and political events, and shifts in investor psychology.

Most investors know they are supposed to be factoring risk and return in making investment decisions. Unfortunately, evaluating investment risk is more complex and less certain than many investors would like. Risk is often equated with the volatility of investment returns. Small-company stocks are said to be riskier than large company stocks, for example, because small company stock returns vary more.

Analysts often measure the standard deviation of the returns from investing in a stock, portfolio of stocks, or mutual fund as an indication of risk. Standard deviation measures the amount by which the actual returns varied from the average return. For instance, if the average annual return for a stock was 20 percent and its standard deviation was 10 percent, then most of the actual returns fell between 10 and 30 percent. A high standard deviation implies greater uncertainty and more risk because returns have varied over a wider range.

Another measure of risk used by professional investors is "beta," a calculation of the volatility of a stock or mutual fund as compared to a broad market indicator such as the Standard & Poor's 500-stock Index. A beta of 1 for a stock or mutual fund means that the stock or fund will move in the same proportion and direction as the S&P 500. A beta of 1.5 implies that the price of a stock or fund will be 50 percent more volatile than the S&P 500. Thus, the higher the beta, the higher the risk.

However, both risk measures have serious flaws. These numbers are calculated using historical returns, but future returns may follow different patterns. As a result, risk measurements often prove to be unreliable.

What should you do to reduce risk and enhance your returns? One strategy has been proven effective at reducing risk without sacrificing return: diversification. Every investor should understand the importance of diversification in reducing risk across different asset classes and across different market environments. Diversification can substantially reduce risk or volatility while sacrificing little in the way of return (see the next Key).

4

DIVERSIFICATION

Everyone should hold between three months and six months of their before tax salary in short-term cash instruments, such as bank deposits and money market funds. But once this level of protection has been reached, you should look for investments that can provide you a return in excess of the rate of inflation. The real return of bank deposits, short-term CDs, and money market funds historically, has been very low after adjusting for inflation and taxes.

Many investors are so intimidated by the gyrations of the stock market that they won't consider anything but fixed-income investments. This strategy will cost them dearly in the long run. Those of you who would like to buy stocks and mutual funds without it affecting your sleep at night should give thought to one of Wall Street's oldest rules: diversify.

Well-diversified portfolios—containing stocks, bonds, real estate, international investments, and so-called cash equivalents like treasury bills and money market funds can substantially reduce the ups and downs of your returns. Research has shown that over lengthy periods, investors have to sacrifice little in the way of returns to get reduced volatility. For example, in the 15-year period from 1980 to 1994, stocks went up at an average compared annual return of 14.52 percent, treasury bonds at 11.17 percent. However, a mixture of 60 percent stocks and 40 percent bonds returned about 13 percent. This return was somewhat less than the return from stocks alone, but the risk of investing only in stocks was substantially reduced.

If you are interested in making the most money possible, and your time horizon is 30 to 40 years, then investing

100 percent in stocks makes sense. Although you have a 30 percent chance of loss in any one-year period (based on results over the last 65 years), your risk drops to 15 percent over any five-year holding period and only 4 percent in any ten-year period. In other words, extending the amount of time invested in the stock market greatly reduces risk.

But most investors have shorter time horizons, and investing totally in stocks is too risky. For them, investing in several classes of assets such as stocks, bonds, real estate (at least your own home), and money market instruments is a better approach.

One diversification strategy that has performed well over the last several decades is the "fixed-mix" approach recommended by Bailard, Biehl & Kaiser, a San Mateo, California investment management firm. Investors using this approach divide their holdings evenly among five types of investments: U.S. stocks, bonds, real estate, cash, and foreign stocks. No-load mutual funds are used to reduce costs. At the end of each year, investors reorganize their holdings so that each holding again comprises about 20 percent of the total. The firm says that this strategy has produced about the same return as U.S. stocks alone at much lower risk since 1966.

Advocates of this fixed-mix approach say that the annual rebalancing does not require the investors to make judgments about market timing. Although this approach has merit, many investors might be uncomfortable investing in areas they know little about such as real estate and foreign stocks.

The best mix of investments will vary depending on your age, income, health, employment stability, family size, inheritances, and tolerance of risk. Each investor has to structure a strategy that fits his own personal circumstances. And this strategy will change as you get older and your financial position changes.

The principle of effective diversification should always be observed. When you buy stocks, don't buy stocks all in the same industries, all small-company stocks, or all resource-based companies. Your portfolio should probably consist of a minimum of 15 different stocks, no two of them in the same industry. Those investors unable to afford 15 different stocks should buy no-load mutual funds.

No-load mutual funds are a terrific way to diversify your portfolio. But here again, don't buy several diffcrent mutual funds that all have the same objective. In buying funds, stick with those with consistent long-term performance. *Money, Fortune, Forbes,* and *Business Week* all periodically evaluate funds and make recommendations. Reduce the risk of stock market fluctuations by hedging with bond funds such as Vanguard Short-Term Federal Bond (800-662-7447).

Those investors exclusively buying mutual funds should be cognizant of the importance of diversification. Mutual funds provide the benefit of diversification because of the large number of securities owned by a typical fund. However, because mutual funds typically specialize in a particular type of asset category such as growth stocks, foreign stocks, small-company stocks, or treasury bonds, the diversification of a given fund is limited to the asset category in which it concentrates.

Diversification among different categories of funds can greatly reduce risk without substantially reducing potential return. One study found that a combination of four categories of mutual funds can achieve a portfolio that has 78 percent less risk than the risk of the average mutual fund category taken alone. Even the simple fixed-mix approach previously discussed offers risk-reduction benefits without substantially affecting return.

One suggestion to improve performance and reduce risk is to allocate 15 to 25 percent of a total fund portfolio to a well-diversified international stock fund. These funds can buy securities in certain foreign economies that are outpacing the growth of domestic securities. Some good choices include T. Rowe Price International Stock (800-638-5660) and Strong International (800-368-1030).

5

FEDERAL RESERVE BOARD

Money is often viewed as the force that moves markets, yet who determines the money supply? This role in our economy is filled by the Federal Reserve Board (the Fed). The Fed is our central bank—the bank that oversees the activities of the over 5,000 commercial banks that are members of the Federal Reserve System. These member banks account for 70 percent of all commercial bank deposits. With its broad supervisory authority over these banks, the Fed also controls the nation's money supply. Because changes in the money supply are so critical to the determination of interest rates and the state of the economy, the Fed is subject to media scrutiny.

Structure of the Fed. At the top of the Fed's organizational structure is the Board of Governors located in Washington. The board consists of seven members appointed by the president of the United States and confirmed by the Senate. All appointments to the board are for 14-year terms. However, the president designates the chairman and the vice-chairman who serve four-year terms with redesignation possible as long as their terms as board members have not expired. The chairman of the board occupies an especially powerful position. The importance of this position is often cited as being second to that of the president.

Implementation of Monetary Policy. Monetary policy refers to the Fed's management of the money supply. The principal tools the Fed can use to regulate the money supply are:

1. *Open-Market Operations.* These operations control the money supply and are the most flexible policy instrument. These operations consist of the

purchase and sale of government securities on the open market. The transactions have a direct impact upon bank reserves and are employed continuously each day as needed.

2. *Discount Window.* Discounting occurs when the Fed lends reserves to member banks. The rate of interest the Fed charges is called the discount rate and it is altered periodically as market conditions change or to complement open market operations. It is primarily of interest as an indication of the Fed's view of the economy and credit demand.

3. *Reserve Requirements.* Banks are required to maintain reserves against the money they lend. When reserve requirements are increased, the amount of deposits supported by the supply of reserves is reduced and banks have to reduce their loans. This tool is the least flexible and is seldom used.

Creation of Money. The money supply is defined as currency in the hands of the public plus transactions accounts in depository institutions and traveler's checks. The Fed and depository institutions are the organizations that determine the money supply. Actually, currency (cash and coins) constitutes only a small percentage of the money supply. The money supply predominantly exists as accounts in banks. Bills are primarily paid with checks or credit cards that are followed by checks. Cash is typically used for small transactions.

How is money created? Very simply, it is created by banks making loans. Assume that a bank makes a loan of $ 100,000 to a company that promises to repay after one year. The bank credits or increases the amount available in the company's checking account. Money supply increases by $100,000 as a result of this transaction. Subsequent repayment is made by deducting $100,000 from the company's checking account. This action reduces the money supply. The principle is simple: making loans increases the money supply, repaying loans reduces it.

What restricts banks' capacity to make loans and create more money? Obviously, when individuals and companies have balances in their checking accounts, they write checks and withdraw cash from their accounts. So banks must maintain reserves either in the form of vault cash or deposits (checking accounts) with the Fed. The Fed requires that banks maintain reserves equal to a specified percentage of their deposits. Deposits are backed by reserves while loans are not. The deposits represent a liability of the bank because the depositors can withdraw their money. The expansion or contraction of deposits increases or decreases the money supply.

Money Supply and Investments. The money supply tends to influence both stock and bond prices through its effect on interest rates and economic activity. Other things being equal, an increase in the rate of growth of the money supply tends to reduce interest rates, making stocks a more attractive investment and bonds less attractive. Meanwhile, a curtailment in the growth rate of the money supply tends to hike interest rates, thus making alternative investments (such as bonds) more appealing than stocks. Obviously, the Fed plays an extremely important role in our financial system. It controls money and has strong influence over whether credit is tight or easy, interest rates are high or low, prices go up or down, and whether the economy is strong or weak. This power is the reason so many "Fed-watchers" exist. The activities of the Fed are under constant scrutiny in the media, and speculation about its motives abound. Since money does drive our markets, it behooves all investors to be aware of the role of the Fed.

6

INTEREST RATES

The interest rate is the price paid for the use of money. Interest is usually expressed as an annual rate or percentage rather than as an absolute amount. Thus, if an individual borrows $1,000 for one year, a payment of $100 on the amount borrowed translates to 10 percent annual interest. Interest rates are usually set by market forces and interest rates charged can differ greatly. A loan to buy a house may cost the borrower 7 to 10 percent annual interest. Department stores and bank charge cards typically charge 18 to 23 percent annual interest. However, the federal government usually pays 4 to 8 percent interest on its debt. Variations in the interest paid result from many factors, including:

1. *Length of loans.* The greater the length of the loan term, the higher the interest rate is. Lenders require a higher return to justify foregoing use of money for longer periods of time.

2. *Risk.* The greater the risk of loan default, the higher the interest rate that will be charged. In addition, a secured loan involves less interest than an unsecured loan since the borrower pledges collateral that can be obtained by the lender in the event of default.

3. *Administrative costs.* Lenders have to expend time and effort to process loans, check references, and process collateral. The larger the amount of the loan, the smaller the administrative costs are as a percentage of the total loan. As a result, larger loans usually command lower interest rates than smaller loans.

Real Versus Nominal Interest Rates. The nominal interest rate is the rate of interest expressed in current

13

dollars. Inflation causes the nominal interest rate to be higher than it would be if there was no inflation. The nominal interest rate rises to reflect the anticipated rate of inflation. The real interest rate is obtained by subtracting the anticipated rate of inflation from the nominal rate of interest. If the nominal rate of interest is 5 percent and the rate of inflation is 5 percent, the real rate of interest is zero.

Panoply of Interest Rates. Although all interest rates tend to move in the same direction at the same time, an examination of the financial pages reveals there are dozens of different interest rates. Some of the most widely quoted interest rates are:

1. *Federal funds rate.* This is the rate banks have to pay to borrow reserves from other banks. A rise in the federal funds rate indicates that more banks are running short of reserves, and a fall indicates the opposite. The federal funds rate also provides an indication of Federal Reserve monetary policy. A rise in the rate signals a more restrictive policy, while a fall indicates a more expansionary policy. However, sharp fluctuations can occur from one day to the next without signaling a change in policy.

2. *Prime rate.* The prime rate is the rate charged by commercial banks to their most creditworthy business customers. Businesses that are less creditworthy are charged a higher interest rate. The prime rate is a bellwether rate in the sense that when it rises all interest rates will rise. Conversely, a reduction in the prime rate signals a decline in all interest rates.

3. *Commercial paper rate.* Commercial paper is unsecured (i.e., no collateral) debt issued by the largest corporations. Corporations issue commercial paper because the interest will usually be less than that charged by banks.

4. *Consumer loan rate.* This is the rate charged to consumers to borrow money. Interest rates vary depending upon the customer, length of loan term, and type of loan. This rate tends to be considerably higher than the rate on business loans.

5. *Mortgage rate.* The mortgage rate is charged by thrift institutions to home buyers. Up to 90 percent of the cost of a home is usually borrowed and repaid in monthly installments over 20 to 30 years. A climb in mortgage rates raises monthly payments and has a depressing effect on new home construction.

6. *Treasury bill rate.* These short-term securities mature in three months, six months, or one year and are issued in minimum denominations of $ 10,000 with $5,000 increments. Treasury bills are sold at a discount from face value and are redeemed at full face value upon maturity. Since they are guaranteed by the full faith and credit of the U.S. government, they are the safest of securities.

7. *Long-term bond rate.* Interest rates depend upon the length of the bond term and the creditworthiness of the issuer. Bonds that mature in 30 years pay a higher rate than bonds maturing in ten years. The reason is that price fluctuates with changes in the level of interest rates, increasing the risk of capital loss over the longer term. Inflation expectation is also built in. Treasury bonds pay less interest than corporate bonds because the probability of repayment is nearly certain. Treasury bonds mature in 30 years and are issued in $1,000 minimum denominations with $5,000, $10,000, $50,000, $100,000, and $1 million denominations also available.

Changes in interest rates affect almost all investments. For example, a rise in interest rates makes bonds more attractive, shifting capital from stocks to bonds. Conversely, lower interest rates make bonds less attractive, and money shifts from debt instruments to investments in common stock.

7

SAVINGS ACCOUNTS

A savings account is an account in a depository institution such as a bank, savings and loan, or credit union that permits frequent deposit or withdrawal of funds and assesses no fees as long as a low minimum balance is maintained. Since a passbook was once used to record transactions in these accounts, they are called passbook accounts, and their rate of interest is called the passbook rate. Passbooks are generally not issued today; instead, many banks have substituted the statement account, which provides a printed monthly or quarterly financial statement from the bank. Statement account holders are provided printed receipts to evidence the account transactions.

Savings accounts are referred to as time deposits because they are expected to remain on deposit longer than demand deposits (checks). A statement account typically has a higher minimum deposit requirement than the $1 to $50 required to open a passbook account. Accounts with average balances of less than a specified amount are typically assessed a quarterly maintenance fee. Inactive accounts (no deposit or withdrawal within a specified period, such as a year) are usually assessed a service charge.

Savings accounts in recent years have paid an interest rate of about 3 percent. Banks often advertise the annual rate as well as the effective yield. The difference between the two reflects how often interest is credited to your account. A 3 percent interest rate has an effective annual yield of 3 percent if interest is credited annually. If interest is credited quarterly, the annual yield becomes 3.058 percent, and if it is credited monthly, the annual yield goes up to 3.067 percent.

Little reason exists to have a savings account unless you are opening an account for a child. A 3 percent return means your capital is being eroded by inflation and taxes. Other alternatives such as an insured money market account with a bank are just as safe and accessible, and they pay a substantially higher return. Incredibly, over $400 billion is still languishing in low-interest savings accounts. Many depositors are not aware of how their savings are being eroded by inflation and taxes, and banks are delighted to have this low-cost money on deposit.

With the widespread publicity about the financial difficulties of banks and savings and loans, many depositors are concerned about the safety of their money. This concern is unwarranted if your money is in a financial institution that is federally insured. The vast majority of commercial banks savings and loans, savings banks, and credit unions are federally insured by U.S. government agencies. If your bank or savings and loan fails, you will get your money back. The safety of your funds is guaranteed up to a maximum of $100,000 per depositor held in a single institution. Remember that the deposit insurance applies to each depositor and not to the deposit account. Therefore, both the checking and savings accounts of each depositor are insured, and as long as the maximum insurable amount is not exceeded, the depositor can have any number of accounts and still be fully protected.

Some institutions are insured by state or private deposit insurance. Most experts believe that these institutions provide less protection against loss than do the federally insured ones. The best bet is to stick with Uncle Sam.

8

NOW ACCOUNTS

Checking accounts held at a bank are technically known as demand deposits, meaning that the withdrawal of funds must be allowed whenever demanded by the depositor. You put money into your checking account by depositing funds and withdraw it by writing checks.

Regular checking is the most common type of checking account. The account does not pay interest and will not assess monthly and transaction fees as long as a minimum balance is maintained. Current law permits only banks to offer regular checking.

Commercial banks, savings and loans institutions (S&Ls), savings banks, and credit unions can offer depositors another kind of checking account called a negotiable order of withdrawal (NOW) account or, in the case of credit unions, share draft accounts. These accounts pay about the same interest as passbook savings accounts, about 3 percent. There is no legal minimum balance for a NOW account, but many institutions impose their own requirements such as an initial minimum deposit of $2,500. To earn interest, a certain minimum balance must be maintained.

You should be careful and understand all the rules and fees in selecting a bank. One of the major problems of interest-paying checking accounts has been a rise in monthly bank charges that often wipes out any interest earned.

A NOW account can be a good choice if you maintain the minimum balance and avoid the charges. If you have difficulty maintaining the minimum balance, a regular checking account is often a better choice. NOW accounts should be viewed primarily as checking accounts that provide a chance to earn interest. As such, they allow you to earn interest on balances that must be kept for transaction purposes and would otherwise lie idle.

9

MONEY MARKET DEPOSIT ACCOUNTS

A money market deposit account (MMDA) is a government-insured money market account offered through a depository institution such as a bank, credit union, or savings and loan association. MMDAs were created so that these institutions could compete for deposits with money market funds. MMDAs pay the highest rate of any bank account on which checks can be written.

MMDAs have minimum-balance requirements, often $2,500. If your average monthly balance falls below the minimum, the entire account earns interest at the rate of a regular NOW account, about 3 percent. Depositors are typically limited to six transactions per month (only three by check) before withdrawal fees are assessed. Each account is insured by the appropriate federal agency (FDIC for banks, FSLIC for S&Ls) for $100,000.

Depositors like these accounts because of their convenience and safety. The interest rates paid may be about 1 percent higher than passbook savings rates, .5 to 2 percent lower than the best-managed money market mutual funds, and generally .5 percent below that of treasury bills. Although money market mutual funds offer significantly higher returns as well as check-writing privileges, many depositors like the extra margin of safety provided by the government-insured MMDA accounts.

It pays to shop around for a MMDA because rates and fees can vary. A MMDA in an out-of-town bank paying higher interest rates makes sense as long as you have easy access to cash in a local account. Information on MMDA yields is available in many newspapers, the Sunday edition of *The New York Times, Barron's*, and the "Your Money Monitor" column in *Money* magazine.

10

U.S. SAVINGS BONDS

Savings bonds used to be a joke in the investment world. Patriotism was used as the lure to attract investors while the bonds provided very low interest rates. These were the investments of choice by low-income families and were ignored by sophisticated investors.

But since 1982, U.S. Savings Bonds have been revamped to make them more attractive to investors. Savings bonds are now one of the simplest, safest, and most effective ways to build a nest egg. These days holders can expect decent (if unspectacular) returns, similar to those on certificates of deposit or money market funds.

Savings bonds are especially appropriate for people who have difficulty putting away money for goals such as retirement. They can be purchased through the payroll-deduction plans offered by many companies. Since you don't see the money, after a while you may not miss it.

Cost and Return. A Series EE Savings Bond is an appreciation-type security that is issued for an original maturity of 12 years and is available in denominations of $50, $75, $100, $200, $500, $1,000, $5,000, and $10,000. The purchase price is one-half the denomination; for example, a $100 bond costs $50. They may be purchased at most commercial banks, many savings institutions, and through the payroll savings plan offered by thousands of employers.

A Series EE Savings Bond is a contract showing that money has been loaned to the United States, which promises to repay it with accrued interest when the bond is redeemed. Bonds are safe and secure because they are backed by the full faith and credit of the U.S. government. There is no sales commission and the minimum purchase is only $25.

Previously, Series EE Bonds issued on or after November 1, 1982 and held at least five years earned interest at a variable market-based rate or a minimum rate, whichever was more. The Treasury has recently made the biggest changes since the minimum interest rate was started in 1976. As of May 1, 1995, all savings bonds have variable interest rates linked to the rates on Treasury bills and notes, and the guaranteed minimum rate, which was 4 percent, disappeared for bonds held less than 17 years.

Every May 1 and November 1, the Treasury will announce:

1. A short-term interest rate that is 85 percent of the average yield on six month Treasury bills the previous three months. All savings bonds will earn this rate their first five years.
2. A long-term rate that is 85 percent of the average yield on five-year Treasury notes the previous six months. All savings bonds five years or older earn the higher rate until they reach face value.

The Treasury guarantees that all bonds can be redeemed for full face value after 17 years. Essentially, that means a guaranteed return of slightly more than 4 percent if a bond is held the full 17 years. To estimate when your bond may reach face value, use the Rule of 72: divide 72 by the current interest rate. The result is the number of years it would take for any investment to double at that interest rate.

Savings bonds have significant tax advantages. Like other U.S. obligations, savings bonds pay interest that is free from state and local taxes. Owners can choose between paying federal income tax on the accrued interest each year or taking the deferral until redemption—a maximum of 30 years. Interest on savings bonds isn't paid out periodically but rather as a lump sum when a bond is redeemed.

Education Benefit. The interest on Series EE Savings Bonds—already exempt from state and local income tax—may be exempt from federal income tax if you pay tuition and fees at colleges, universities, and qualified technical schools during the year you redeem the bonds. To qualify for the interest exclusion, the bonds must be issued after December 31, 1989 to individuals who are at least 24 years old. If the bonds are intended to benefit dependent children, they must be issued in either one parent's name or both parents' names—the bonds cannot be issued in the name of a child. The bonds must be redeemed in a year that the bond owner pays qualified educational expenses to an eligible educational institution. Only tuition and fees are qualified educational expenses—not room and board.

The interest on qualifying bonds will be fully exempt from federal income tax only if the qualifying tuition and fees paid during the year are equal to or more than the redemption proceeds (interest and principal). If tuition and fees are less than the value of the bonds cashed, the exemption is proportional to the percentage of the value that was used for tuition and fees. For example, if you redeem $10,000 worth of bonds during the year but tuition and fees total only $8,000, 80 percent of the interest income is exempt from federal income tax.

Income limits apply to the year of redemption of the bonds. In 1995, if you are/were single with an adjusted gross income of $57,300 or less or a married couple filing a joint return with an income of $63,450 or less, you may be entitled to a full exemption. (Married taxpayers filing separately are not eligible for the exemption.)

Series HH Savings Bonds are current-income securities. When Series EE Savings Bonds mature, the proceeds can be reinvested in Series HH Savings Bonds and taxes further deferred until the HH bonds mature in ten years. HH Bonds are issued and redeemed at face value, with interest paid semiannually by the Treasury Department. Series HH Bonds can only be issued in exchange for Series EE Bonds that have reached maturity.

Information on savings bonds is available from the Department of the Treasury, U.S. Savings Bond Marketing Office, Washington, DC 20226, Telephone: 202-377-7715.

For current rates on savings bonds, call 800-872-6637.

11

CERTIFICATE OF DEPOSIT (CD)

CDs are a safe, simple, and popular way to invest surplus cash for periods that range from one month to five years. CDs are time certificates sold by banks, savings and loan institutions (S&Ls), and credit unions for minimum amounts of $500 to $1,000. You deposit the money with the institution, and they in return agree to pay you a specified interest rate. When the CD matures, you get the full amount you left on deposit plus interest.

Normally, the longer the money is left on deposit, the higher the interest rate will be. Interest on six-month CDs is comparable to what is generally paid by money market mutual funds, while the longer-term CDs will usually pay about 1 percent more than treasury securities of comparable maturity.

CDs are safe because all deposits in banks and savings and loans are federally insured to $100,000. It pays to shop around because banks and S&Ls pay different CD rates. Most large-circulation newspapers carry weekly CD rates. The Sunday edition of *The New York Times* and the weekly edition of *Barron's* are also excellent sources. In addition, the Wednesday edition of *The Wall Street Journal* provides a listing of the nation's highest-yielding CDs. Finally, *Money* provides a ranking of the financial standing of the banks providing the highest-yielding CDs in its "Your Money Monitor" section of the magazine.

Searching for the highest available rates on CDs might not be worth the effort it once was. The highest CD rates are typically paid by banks and savings and loans on the weakest financial footing. You should be cautious and stay clear of troubled S&Ls. Although your money is insured up to $100,000, if the institution is closed for liquidation, there may be delays in getting your money back. In addition, you may not be able to reinvest your funds at the same rate. In other words, go with a healthy bank or S&L.

Although financial health can be difficult to determine, some services will provide you with a "best estimate" of health based upon past statistics. For $10, Veribanc Inc. (800-442-2657) will provide you with a rating of a bank's safety. The same service is provided by Weiss Research for $10 (800-289-8100).

Penalties and Interest. Remember to always ask your bank about its policy regarding penalties for cashing in a CD before it matures. Although banks are usually willing to remit your full deposit before a CD matures, they always specify an interest penalty on cash that is prematurely withdrawn. CDs of a year or less charge an interest penalty of one month's interest.

Before buying any CD, make sure you understand the interest rate you are receiving. Some CDs compound interest daily, others weekly, and still others quarterly. The more frequent the compounding, the greater the interest you receive. For comparison purposes, the key value is the "effective annual yield." A CD paying a 6 percent interest rate that compounds annually pays an effective annual yield of 6 percent. The same interest rate compounded daily has an effective annual yield of 6.28 percent. Remember to always ask for the effective annual yield.

Broker CDs. Some of the best deals on bank CDs aren't available at banks. Large brokerage firms offer rates on bank CDs that are often a full percentage point higher than the rates offered by many major banks. Brokerage firms buy huge CDs of $100,000 or more and then sell them to individual investors in smaller units. Broker CDs carry the same federal insurance on deposits up to $100,000 and are typically easier to cash in early than those offered by banks and S&Ls. Further, you don't pay your broker a commission since the bank pays the broker to sell the CD.

Buying a CD from a brokerage firm permits you to comparison shop with one phone call. Instead of making numerous telephone inquiries to banks located in different states, you can get a list of high-yielding CDs in a single call or visit. Be sure to ask for Standard & Poor's rating of a CD, if available, when the yield is quoted to you. Generally, issuers with CDs that have been given the lowest credit ratings are considered to be the least creditworthy. Of course the risk associated with such a purchase is not of the same order as the risk associated with a speculative stock or bond because your CD is subject to federal deposit insurance.

In an effort to obtain higher interest rates than CDs pay, many investors have purchased instruments called "subordinated debt notes" or "lobby notes," sold by banks and S&Ls. When you buy these instruments, you are lending money to the institution. Lobby notes are not protected by federal deposit insurance. If the institution goes bankrupt, your investment will likely be worthless.

These instruments are often sold by banks and S&Ls that are in relatively poor financial condition. However, even if the institution doesn't fail, you can still get shafted. Lobby notes often contain provisions allowing the bank to redeem them before the full term expires. The high interest income you expected might be lost before the expiration of the term.

These instruments should be avoided by conservative investors. If you are tempted, call Veribanc for a financial-soundness rating on the institution. If the rating is less than three-stars, forget it.

12

TREASURY SECURITIES

The largest fixed-income market in the world is that for U.S. Treasury obligations. The federal government issues debt obligations that are backed by the full faith and credit of the U.S. government and, therefore, offer the investor maximum safety of principal and a guaranteed yield. Although the yield is typically less than a corporate bond, treasury securities are the closest approximation to risk-free investments.

The three most popular treasury securities for individual investors are treasury bills, treasury notes, and treasury bonds. Treasury bills have maturities up to and including one year. Treasury notes mature in two to ten years, while treasury bonds mature in 30 years. The process of selling these securities to the public initially takes place in the primary market (market for new issues), and proceeds go to the Treasury Department.

Treasury Bills (T-bills). T-bills are offered by the Treasury with maturities of three, six, or twelve months. These securities are issued every Monday in minimum denominations of $10,000 and in increments of $5,000 above the minimum. Investors bid for them at a discount by offering, for example, $99 for every $100 of T-bills. At maturity, the investor will receive $100. Yields are expressed on an annual basis, so that in the case of a three-month T-bill purchased for $99, the yield would be the discount of $1 divided by the price of $99 and multiplied by four because there are four three-month periods in a year. For this example, the yield would be 4.04 percent. The gain of $1 is interest income and subject to federal income tax but is exempt from state and local taxes.

Treasury Notes (T-Notes). Treasury issues maturing between two and ten years are called T-notes. They are issued in $1,000 and $5,000 denominations with a fixed interest rate determined by the coupon rate specified in the note. The interest earned is paid semiannually and, like T-bills, exempt from state and local taxes.

T-notes have several characteristics that account for their increasing popularity. One is that the $1,000 minimum makes them more affordable than T-bills that are issued in minimum denominations of $10,000. Another plus is that their longer maturities usually mean a greater return for investors than T-bills can provide.

Treasury Bonds (T-bonds). These securities make up the smallest segment of the federal debt. These bonds mature and repay their face value after 30 years from the date of issue. They are issued in denominations of $1,000, $5,000, $10,000, $50,000, $100,000 and $1 million. A fixed rate of interest is paid semiannually and the interest earned is exempt from state and local taxes. Some of these issues are callable or redeemable prior to maturity. A callable bond is indicated in the newspaper by a hyphen between the call date and the maturity date. For instance, if 2000–2004 is listed under "maturity" in a newspaper, that means the bond can be redeemed at any time starting in 2000.

Buying Treasuries. Treasury securities can be bought at any time by contacting your broker. If you want to save the minimum broker's fee of $50 to $75, you can buy treasuries directly from Uncle Sam through the mail or in person under the Treasury Direct program. The number of individual accounts in the Treasury Direct purchase program has grown to more than two million. Buying directly from the Treasury is most appropriate for people who plan to keep the securities until they mature. Treasuries can be sold on the secondary market (market where securities are sold after their original issuance) but only through a broker or bank, which involves a commission.

When buying directly at auction, most individuals elect to be "noncompetitive bidders." This bid guarantees you the average yield of the successful bids from institutional investors. You can also buy all the securities you want at this average yield. To buy directly, you have to wait for an auction. In recent years this schedule has been followed:

- 13-week and 26-week T-bills are auctioned every Monday (Tuesday if Monday is a holiday).
- 52-week bills are auctioned every four weeks, usually on a Thursday.
- 2-year and 5-year notes are auctioned at the end of each month.
- 3-year and 10-year notes are auctioned two times a year.
- 30-year bonds are auctioned four times a year.

Bids may be submitted in person to any of the 37 Federal Reserve banks or branches until 1:00 P.M. EST on the day of the auction. Bids sent by mail must be postmarked no later than the day before the auction. To find out when and where to buy treasuries, you can call your local Federal Reserve bank or branch, or the Bureau of Public Debt's information number: 202-874-4000.

Anyone interested in the Treasury Direct purchase program should first obtain the free packet of information by writing: "Treasury Direct," Bureau of Public Debt, Dept. F, Washington DC 20239-1200. A comprehensive discussion of Treasury securities can be obtained by sending a check for $4.50 payable to the Federal Reserve Bank of Richmond, P.O. Box 27471, Richmond, VA 23261, and asking for *Buying Treasury Securities.*

Although treasuries are the safest possible investment (and interest is exempt from state and local taxes), remember that you still face market risk. If market interest rates go up, the market value of your security will drop. Of course, if you hold the security until maturity, you are guaranteed to receive its face value.

13

COMMON STOCK

Common stock represents units of ownership in a corporation. Owners of common stock bear the ultimate risk of loss and reap the benefits of success. Upon dissolution neither dividends nor assets are guaranteed to common stockholders. But common stockholders are the owners of the corporation and will profit more than bondholders if the company is successful.

Preferred stock is distinguished from common stock because it has certain preferential rights. Preferred stockholders have priority in the receipt of dividend income and claims on company assets in case of dissolution. The benefits of investing in preferred stock are similar to those of bonds. Preferred stock dividends are usually paid at a fixed rate. Most preferred stock dividends are cumulative, so that omitted dividends are accumulated and paid in total before common stock dividends can be paid.

Although preferred stock provides for reduced risk, its price typically has more modest potential for capital gains than common stock. Because corporate investors enjoy an exclusion from taxes on preferred dividends, they (more than individuals) are the buyers of preferred issues. The most popular way to invest in corporations is to own shares of common stock. More than 60 million individuals own shares in a publicly traded company or stock mutual fund.

Advantages of Common Stock. Common stock has certain advantages that make it an attractive investment:

1. *Liquidity.* Most common stocks traded on stock exchanges can be quickly bought or sold at or near the prior day prices that are quoted in the financial press. If the price of stock goes up, the investor can instruct a broker to sell the stock at a specific price

or at "market," which is the best price attainable at the time of trade. Alternatively, if stock goes down, the investor can sell immediately to cut losses. It will take five working days to complete the transaction, but the transaction price can be quickly obtained from a broker. The stock markets provide liquidity for securities by bringing together sellers and buyers. The ease of transfer is one of the great advantages of trading in common stock over alternative investments such as physical real estate.

2. *Dividends.* Dividends are important to investors who want ever-increasing income. Dividends are declared on a per share basis and typically paid quarterly in cash. A stock that has a $2-per-share cash dividend means that 50 cents per share will be paid every three months on each share of stock. Quality companies periodically increase dividends as earning levels increase over time.

Dividends become a liability of the corporation when they are formally declared by the board of directors. Until that action is taken, a corporation has no responsibility to pay common stock dividends. Typically, corporations are reluctant to cut or eliminate the dividend even if profits decline for fear of raising the ire of stockholders. However, profits are the primary determinants of dividends, and ultimately, rising dividends will only result from rising profits.

Not all corporations distribute dividends to shareholders. Frequently, smaller corporations need to husband their cash for reinvestment purposes and will not distribute cash to stockholders. Even large corporations face cash shortages. Under these circumstances, instead of distributing cash, corporations may issue additional shares of stock. The investor's equity ownership is unaltered by a stock dividend. For example, if an investor owns 1,000 shares of stock in a corporation with total stock outstanding of 100,000 shares, the investor owns 1 percent of that corporation. After a stock dividend of 10 percent, the investor will still own 1 percent of the corporation—1,100 shares out of a total of 110,000 shares. A stock dividend merely breaks the total pie down into smaller pieces without changing real ownership interest. Investors typically buy stock that pays little or no dividends if their interest is in capital gains.

3. *Capital appreciation.* Many investors are less interested in dividends than in seeing the price of their stock appreciate. In fact wealthy investors may desire that dividends not be paid. The earnings not distributed to stockholders in dividends represent tax-deferred income. The reinvestment of profits should help the company earn greater profits in the future. Other things being equal, the greater the earnings or profits in the future, the more likely the stock is to appreciate in price. Furthermore, taxes are not paid on gains until the stock is sold.

Common Stock Compared to Other Investments. Many investors see the stock market move up and down, become alarmed, and view it as too risky for the individual investor. They are making a mistake. In August 1995, the average current rate on one-year CDs was only 5.14 percent. Taking into consideration inflation and taxes, the real return (return adjusted for inflation) was about 1 percent.

What's the best place to park your long-term money? The bulk of your long-term investments should be placed into a diversified portfolio of carefully selected stocks or stock-owning mutual funds. According to Ibbotson Associates in Chicago, stocks have produced a return of 6.9 percent over the rate of inflation since 1926. This return far exceeds the inflation adjusted return of 1.7 percent for long-term government bonds. Although stocks can be risky in the short run, no investment is better for the small investor in the long run (ten years or more).

14

BLUE CHIPS AND OTHER TYPES OF STOCKS

Investors frequently describe stocks by categorizing them according to risk and return characteristics. Although these classifications are useful, investors should remember that there are no guarantees in the stock market. Stocks of prominent companies can often be major disappointments. Bethlehem Steel continues to sell below the high of $60 it reached in the 1950s. No stock is always an excellent holding, and every investment involves risk. Investors should remember that a stock classified as a growth stock may rapidly change to a speculative stock and vice versa. With this caveat in mind, stocks are frequently classified in the following categories: blue chip stocks, growth stocks, cyclical stocks, defensive stocks, and speculative stocks.

Blue Chip Stocks. Blue chip stocks are shares of common stock in a nationally known company that has a long history of profit growth and dividend payments. Some examples of blue chip stocks include General Electric, Coca-Cola, and Exxon. Blue chip stocks tend to be relatively high priced and to pay a low dividend relative to their price because investors are willing to pay more for the lower risk associated with owning these stocks. These companies are frequently involved in multiple industries or in different segments of the same industry.

Many investors associate blue chip stocks with the stocks that comprise the Dow Jones Industrial Average, the well-known market index of 30 large companies listed on the New York Stock Exchange. The names of the stocks that comprise this index are listed daily in *The Wall Street Journal* and *Investor's Business Daily*.

Growth Stocks. Growth stocks represent ownership in companies that have had, and are expected to continue to have, consistently superior earnings growth. These companies typically provide little dividend income since earnings are largely reinvested to finance future growth. *The Value Line Investment Survey* provides listings of growth stock (stocks they define as having provided superior growth over the last ten years). Growth stocks are more likely to be found in the over-the-counter market since it is easier for companies to grow rapidly from a smaller base.

Although it is tempting to look for another Microsoft or Intel, investors should be aware of the great risk in investing in growth stocks. By definition, growth stocks are expected to experience above-average growth (earnings for U.S. companies have historically grown at about an average rate of 8 percent per year). If these expectations are realized, investors can earn superior returns. But if the growth does not materialize or if the rate slackens, the stock prices can fall dramatically. Examples of prominent growth stocks include Intel, Microsoft, Berkshire Hathaway, and Compaq Computer.

Cyclical Stocks. Cyclical stocks are stocks in an industry that is very responsive to the business cycle. Their earnings and stock prices can decline dramatically as the economy weakens and, correspondingly, strengthen as the economy picks up steam. Because their earnings tend to fluctuate more, cyclical stocks usually are riskier and more volatile than blue chip or defensive stocks. Stocks of noncyclical companies such as banks, food, and drugs are not as affected by changes in the business cycle. Among the cyclical industries are auto, steel, copper, aluminum, machinery, and housing.

Defensive Stocks. Defensive stocks are stocks in companies that are relatively immune to the ups and downs of the economy. These stocks have continually stable earnings in comparison with other stocks. Their prices tend to fluctuate less than prices of other stocks. These stocks are less risky than cyclical stocks. The stability in their earnings is accounted for by the relatively stable market for their products. Examples of defensive stock groups include tobacco, food, and drugs. Investors should consider these stocks when anticipating market downturns.

Speculative Stocks. Investments in speculative stocks offer a relatively large chance for a loss and a small chance for a large gain. Of course, a speculative stock is not automatically a bad investment. Usually, there is a small probability of very substantial returns. A sophisticated investor may be willing to assume the greater risk in the hope of generating substantial returns. An investment in an oil exploration stock would be an example. However, this type of stock should represent only a small proportion of an investor's portfolio—and the investor should have sufficient means so that any loss sustained would not mean financial hardship.

Stocks without a long-term record of profitability are questionable investments at any time. The penny-stock market is an example of a market to be approached with the utmost caution. The North American Securities Administrators Association reports that penny-stock swindles cost investors at least $2 billion a year and are the "number-one threat" to small investors in the United States.

15

STOCK EXCHANGES

Common stocks are traded primarily on nine stock exchanges in the United States. The largest one is the New York Stock Exchange (NYSE), which includes 2,547 companies with more than 220 billion shares authorized and a market value of about $5 trillion. A smaller version of the NYSE is the American Stock Exchange (AMEX), which is also located in Manhattan's financial district. These two are considered national exchanges. Common stock is also traded on seven major regional exchanges.

Trading Activity. The number of shares listed as well as the number of shares traded on the NYSE has increased steadily through the years. Prior to the 1960s, the average daily trading volume was less than three million shares. Daily volume averaged about 15 million shares during the first half of the 1970s and exceeded 30 million by the end of the decade. By 1990, daily volume was exceeding 150 million shares, and currently, daily volume exceeds 300 million shares. The NYSE expects daily volume to exceed a trillion shares in the upcoming decade. On October 20, 1987, a record volume of 608,120,000 shares was traded on the NYSE.

Trading volume on the AMEX typically varies from 5 percent to 7 percent of that on the NYSE. The disparity between the activity on the two exchanges is greater when measured by the value of trading because the price of shares on the NYSE tends to be higher than that of shares on the AMEX.

Originally, regional exchanges traded the securities of the companies located in their areas—thus the origin of the name. However, the development of rapid communication expanded their scope. As a result, regional exchanges now trade some NYSE and AMEX stocks as well as local stocks. The largest of the regionals is the

Chicago Stock Exchange. Its trading volume in dollars now exceeds that of the AMEX, making it the second largest organized stock exchange in the United States.

Role of the Specialist. Stock exchange specialists are the center of the auction market for stocks. Their role is critical in maintaining an orderly market for stocks. Specialists are members of the exchange, each of whom has been assigned responsibility for about 15 different stocks. They must possess substantial capital and the knowledge to carry out their responsibilities. Currently, there are about 400 specialists on the NYSE.

In their effort to maintain fair and orderly markets in stocks assigned to them, specialists perform four distinct roles:

1. *Agent:* Specialists act as agents for other brokers on the floor.
2. *Dealer:* Specialists are also required to act as dealers, risking their own capital whenever a temporary imbalance between buy and sell orders exists in any of their assigned stocks.
3. *Auctioneer:* In addition to quoting the current bid and asked price to other brokers, they also evaluate the orders they hold and establish a fair market price for each assigned stock at the beginning of each trading day.
4. *Catalyst:* Finally, specialists are supposed to serve as the market's catalysts, ensuring that orders in their assigned stocks move smoothly.

The performance of the specialists on the exchange has been the source of great controversy. Many critics complain that specialists are more concerned with trading for their own accounts than with maintaining a fair and orderly market. Criticism was heightened by the "crash" on October 19, 1987 (the market dropped 22.6 percent) when trading in many stocks was halted. Currently, block trades involving large lots of stock are handled not by the specialists on the floor of the exchange but by a negotiated sale through brokerage houses or investment banks.

16

OVER-THE-COUNTER MARKET

The term over-the-counter (OTC) originated when securities were traded over the counters in stores of various dealers from their inventory of securities. However, the term is currently an inaccurate description of how securities are traded in this market. The OTC market does not have centralized trading floors where all orders are processed, as do the New York Stock Exchange (NYSE) and the American Stock Exchange (AMEX). Instead, trading is conducted through a centralized computer-telephone network linking dealers across the country. These systems allow dealers to deal directly with one another and with customers.

The OTC market is a negotiated market in which securities are bought and sold through dealers, who buy and sell securities for their own accounts. The number of dealers that make a market in a particular security depends upon the popularity and the size of the issue. Each dealer making a market in a security, purchases securities from sellers at a bid price while selling to buyers at a higher asked price. The difference between the bid and asked price is the spread that represents the dealer's profit.

When an investor trades OTC, an order is presented to a broker. If the broker acts as a dealer in that security, the broker will fill the order from inventory. Otherwise, the broker will act as an agent in contacting the dealer who offers the best price. The broker usually charges a commission for finding the dealer who makes a market in the security.

Securities Traded. The OTC market is a huge market including about 30,000 securities. Although OTC stocks represent many small and unseasoned companies, the range of securities traded is actually great. The types of securities traded include common and preferred stocks, corporate bonds, U.S. government securities, municipal bonds, options and warrants, and foreign securities.

There are several reasons why some securities are represented in the OTC market rather than being listed on one of the exchanges. Some securities issued by smaller companies cannot meet the more stringent requirements of the exchanges. Unseasoned issues of smaller companies typically are traded in the OTC market. In many cases, they will eventually qualify for listing on one of the exchanges.

In other cases, firms choose to have their securities traded in the OTC market even though they could fulfill the requirements for listing on the exchanges. Sometimes this occurs because management prefers the negotiated OTC market, with its multiple dealers making a market in stocks, rather than the specialist system offered by the organized exchanges. Other companies may wish to avoid the financial disclosure and reporting requirements of the exchanges. Many large financial institutions continue to prefer to trade their securities in the OTC market.

NASDAQ. Prior to 1971, OTC quotations were compiled daily by the National Quotations Bureau (a private company), which published this data on what are commonly called "pink sheets." A major problem with this approach was the difficulty in getting current quotations from dealers. A broker had to contact various dealers to determine which one offered the best price for the investor—an inefficient and time-consuming approach.

In 1971, the NASD started providing automated quotations through its National Association of Securities Dealers Automatic Quotations (NASDAQ) system. This computerized communication network provides current bid and asked prices on more than 5,600 securities. Through a terminal, a broker can instantly learn the bid and asked quotations of all dealers making a market in a stock and can then contact the dealer that offers the best price and negotiate a trade directly through terminals.

NASDAQ has been extremely successful. Its dollar trading volume makes it the third largest secondary securities market in the world, surpassed only by the dollar volume on the NYSE and the Tokyo Stock Exchange. The daily trading volume on NASDAQ exceeds that of the NYSE. (NASDAQ stocks sell at an average price per share significantly below the shares on the NYSE.)

NASDAQ Listing Requirements. NASDAQ has minimum requirements that must be met before securities can be traded, but these requirements are not as stringent as those of the NYSE . For companies to be initially listed, they must have $4 million in total assets and $2 million of stockholders' equity. In addition, at least 300 stockholders must hold 100,000 outstanding shares, and at least two dealers must make a market in the shares. Foreign common stocks have different listing requirements.

Buying OTC Stocks. When you see quotes for OTC stock in the newspaper, you will notice two prices for each stock. The bid (or lower) price is what the brokers or dealers are offering to pay for the stock. The higher (or asked) price is the price at which brokers or dealers will sell the stock. The difference between these two amounts is called the spread; it represents the broker's or dealer's profit for selling the stock. The more active the trading in the stock, the narrower the spread tends to be. Inactively traded stocks can have spreads that exceed 20 percent. This means that the stock you purchase has a market value, if sold immediately, that is 20 percent less than its cost.

Penny stock (stocks that typically sell for less than $5 a share) often have spreads exceeding 25 percent. These stocks should be avoided by conservative investors. Billions have been lost by buying penny stocks. This market has been particularly subject to fraud and manipulation.

17

DIVIDENDS

Dividends are distributions of earnings to stockholders. Although most commonly in the form of cash or stock, dividends can also consist of property such as merchandise, real estate, or investments. In most cases, corporations can only declare dividends out of earnings, although some state laws and corporate agreements permit the declaration of dividends from sources other than earnings. Dividends based on sources other than earnings are sometimes described as liquidating dividends because they are a return of the stockholder's investment rather than profits.

Cash Dividends. Cash dividends are the portion of earnings or profits distributed to stockholders in the form of cash. They become a liability of the corporation after the board of directors properly approves or declares their future payment. Cash dividends are usually paid on a quarterly basis shortly after the dividend resolution has been approved by the board of directors. Dividends cannot be paid immediately because the ongoing purchases and sales of the corporation's stock require that a current list of stockholders be prepared. For example, a resolution approved at the April 10 (declaration date) meeting of the board of directors might be declared payable on May 5 (payment date) to all stockholders of record as of April 25 (record date). The period from April 10 to April 25 provides time for any transfers in process to be completed and registered with the transfer agent. Investors owning the stock as of April 25 receive the dividend even if the stock was sold between April 25 and the date of payment, May 5. Therefore, on the day after the record date, the stock trades "ex-dividend" and usually falls slightly in price to compensate for the fact that it no longer qualifies for the latest dividend.

Dividend Yield. The dividend yield percentage is often reported in the stock tables of major newspapers. This number is obtained by dividing the annual cash dividend by the closing price of the stock. The annual cash dividend is based upon the rate of the last quarterly payout. If the dividend in the last quarter was 25 cents per share, the annual dividend is assumed to be $1.00. This number can be compared with the yield of other stocks and with the interest paid on debt instruments.

Stock Splits and Stock Dividends. A stock split is the issuance to stockholders of new shares of stock. For example, a 2-for-1 split gives each stockholder two new shares for each one of the old shares. In effect, a stock dividend is simply a small stock split. For example, if a corporation issues a 5 percent stock dividend, the owner of 100 shares will receive an additional five shares of stock. Essentially, all that happens with these operations is that the total number of shares outstanding increases, the price per share decreases proportionately, and the total value of the owners' common stock remains unchanged. If nothing is to be gained through stock dividends or stock splits, what is the motivation behind them? An understood tradition on Wall Street is that absolute stock prices of $25 and $50 are most appealing to investors. Also, stockholders seem to react positively to distributions of additional shares even if the total value of their holdings remains unchanged. Corporations often issue stock dividends when cash dividends are unaffordable. Stock splits often occur following run-ups in the price of the stock.

Importance of Dividends. Many investors ignore dividends and focus on the capital gains they can earn if the stock rises. They look for the stock that can double in value and not the one that produces steadily growing dividends. That could be a mistake. Over the long run one-third to one-half of the total return on stocks comes from dividends. Furthermore buying stocks with a good dividend yield doesn't mean giving up appreciation. Many companies with good dividend records have produced healthy increases in stock prices. Be careful, though, about stocks with exceptionally high dividends. An exceptionally high dividend often means that the price of the stock is depressed for some reason, possibly because the company has undisclosed problems.

For those investors who wish to maximize current income, fixed-income securities produce the highest yields. U.S. Treasury bonds and federally insured certificates of deposit (CDs) issued by banks and thrift institutions are the safest fixed-income securities. Your return is often better on a CD if you buy it directly from a broker.

However, fixed-income securities have a big drawback. Inflation reduces the purchasing power of a fixed stream of funds. At 3 percent inflation, the principal of a bond will lose half its purchasing power in 23 years. In addition, the purchasing power of the interest on bonds declines as well.

The best hedge against inflation in the long run is investment in common stocks directly or through mutual funds. Unlike bonds, stocks have increased their dividend payouts faster than inflation. Common stock dividends tend to increase as a company's sales and profits grow. The return on an 8 percent bond certainly looks more appealing in the current year than the return from a common stock providing a 5 percent dividend yield. However, if the stock' s dividend rises at a 10 percent annual rate, it will equal the bond's yield in six years and keep increasing thereafter.

Mutual funds called equity income funds look for firms that pay relatively high dividends. Some no-load choices with excellent records include Dodge and Cox Stock (800-621-3979) Dreman High Return (800-553-1608), and T. Rowe Price Equity Income (800-638-5660).

18

P/E RATIOS

Is a stock cheap? Is the market undervalued or over-valued? One of the most widely used tools to make this assessment is the price-earnings (P/E) ratio. A P/E ratio is simply a stock's price divided by the company's earnings per share over the most recent four quarters. A high P/E ratio indicates that the market expects exceptional earnings growth, and a low P/E ratio suggests that the market anticipates low earnings growth. The P/E ratio for each stock is listed in the daily stock tables of most major newspapers. Generally, the higher the P/E ratio, the more bullish investors are about a firm's prospects (although abnormally high P/Es of 50 or more often indicate that the company has taken a one-time charge to earnings, skewing the ratio).

P/E and Earnings. The P/E ratio of any stock that is fairly priced should approximately equal the growth rate of earnings. If the P/E of McDonald's is 15, an investor would expect the company's earnings to be growing at about 15 percent a year. A P/E ratio that is half the growth rate is generally regarded as very positive, and a P/E ratio that is twice the growth rate is usually an unattractive prospect. If you are considering the purchase of a particular stock, it is useful for you to know what you are paying for the earnings compared to what others have paid in the past. The information about earnings growth and P/E histories can be obtained in the Value Line Investment Survey, which is available in most large libraries or from your broker.

High P/E stocks implying high expected future earnings growth can be risky. High P/E stocks experience sharp price drops if earnings don't materialize as expected. Low P/E stocks tend to be less risky because the market has a lower expectation of future earnings growth.

P/E of the Market. The stock market as a whole has its own collective P/E ratio, which is a good indicator of whether the market as a whole is overvalued or undervalued. During the past 50 years the P/E ratio of Standard & Poor's (S&P) 500-stock Index has ranged from seven to more than 40. In August 1987, shortly before the crash of October 1987, the S&P 500-stock Index traded at a P/E ratio of 21 based on the previous four quarters' earnings. The market's overall index had doubled from 1982 to 1987. This increase meant that investors were willing to pay twice as much as what they paid in 1982 for the same corporate earnings—a definite negative sign. Investors should be cautious when the P/E ratio of the S&P 500 exceeds 18. A buying opportunity is definitely signaled when the ratio falls below 12.

Interest rates have a significant effect on the market P/E ratio since investors find stocks more attractive when interest rates are low and bond prices high. Conversely, higher rates make bonds more attractive, shifting money from stocks to fixed income securities. Aside from interest rates, a herd mentality periodically grips the market, driving P/E ratios abnormally high or low. Investors should periodically monitor the P/E ratio of the S&P 500 Index, which is reported on a weekly basis in *Barron's* and in Monday's *The Wall Street Journal*.

19

SELECTING
A BROKER

In buying stocks and bonds, investors must act through a registered broker or dealer. Although these firms are closely regulated by the SEC, it is still important to be careful in selecting a broker, also known as an account executive or registered representative.

No special guidelines are available in selecting a good broker as is true in selecting a good doctor or lawyer. Check with friends, relatives, and business associates for their recommendations. A banker, lawyer, or accountant might also be a source of good information.

You should always arrange for an interview with a prospective broker. Select a time after or before market trading hours when your broker is less likely to be busy. Ask your broker about his or her investment philosophy and professional credentials. Questions you might ask include the following: How long have you been a broker? What is your client base like? Do you primarily recommend conservative investments or do you like to speculate? Do you rely on the recommendations of a research department or do you do your own research? What investment strategy do you favor? If a broker makes extravagant promises, look elsewhere. Keep in mind when dealing with a broker that although brokers like to pose as independent, objective financial advisers, they are primarily salespeople who make their living generating commissions. The reward system is based upon the amount of commissions they earn and not the success of their recommendations to their clients.

You should be sufficiently informed to independently appraise any advice given by your broker. How do you get informed? In addition to reading a daily newspaper, every investor should subscribe to at least one financial periodical such as *Money, Business Week, Forbes,* or *Fortune.* When considering the purchase of stock, check the write-ups in the *Value Line Investment Survey.* A subscription to this publication is expensive but it is available at many local, public, or college libraries.

Full-Service and Discount Brokers. Two kinds of brokers are available to investors. Full-service brokers can provide information about the securities of companies that investors are considering. These brokers are members of firms that typically have research departments that make recommendations and offer advice to their clients. Some of the largest ones are Merrill Lynch, Prudential, and Dean Witter.

Discount brokers simply execute orders employing salaried order clerks who do not receive commissions. They do not make recommendations as to investments. Investors can save 50 to 75 percent on their commissions by using a discount broker.

Investors who use full-service brokers typically do not get their money's worth. A full-service broker will charge a commission of more than $200 on a trade of 500 shares of a $20 stock. The same trade will involve a commission of $50 to $100 at a discount broker. The difference in price has to be justified by the value of the service provided by the full-service broker.

Your full-service broker should be willing to provide you with the details necessary to make informed decisions. Investors should ask for research from the firm's analysts, data on P/E ratios, growth rates, and insider buyer or selling. The broker should also provide Standard & Poor's *Standard Stock Reports* or the *Value Line Investment Survey* reports.

Informed investors should use discount brokers. Examples of discount firms include Charles Schwab (800-435-4000) and Fidelity Brokerage Services (800-225-1799). These firms will charge you half the rate of a full-service broker. While they do not offer investment advice, they do provide services such as checking accounts, 24-hour telephone service, and a large choice of mutual funds.

If you want to cut commissions even further—up to half again as much as a discount broker—several dozen smaller firms known as deep discounters are available. These firms offer low rates because they have found ways to cut costs even more than the well-known discounters. They spend much less on advertising and marketing and offer fewer services. All deep discounters do is buy and sell securities.

Despite the large savings, surprisingly few investors use deep discounters. One reason is that many investors believe deep discounters aren't safe or don't execute orders well. However, these fears are not justified: Almost all interstate brokerage firms—including deep discounters—are covered by SIPC (Securities Investor Protection Corp.), a nonprofit organization established by Congress that insures each customer against failing brokers and security dealers, for holdings up to $500,000, including $100,000 in cash. In addition, order execution should not be a concern since most small-order trades are handled through automated systems. Some deep discount brokerage firms that serve all the states include: Pacific Brokerage Services (800-421-8395), Kennedy Cabot (800-252-0090), First National Brokerage (800-228-3022), Brown (800-225-6707), and Waterhouse Securities (800-421-8300).

Placing an Order. When you decide to purchase stocks or bonds, the first step is to contact a broker and ask for a quote on the security. The quote consists of two numbers: the highest price anyone is currently willing to pay (bid) and the lowest price at which anyone is willing to sell (ask). You have the choice of placing a "market order," which means that you will receive the best price available when the order is executed, or a "limit order," which means the trade can be executed only when (and if) the stock hits a specific price. All orders are day orders unless otherwise indicated. An investor can also choose to place a "good until canceled order," which means the order remains in effect until executed or canceled.

20

STOCK MARKET
TIMING

Is this a good time to buy or sell stocks? This question is the essence of market timing. It would be great if we could buy stocks near the bottom of a declining (or bear) market and sell them near the top of a rising (or bull) market. Unfortunately, the skill of timing the market is possessed by few investors.

The rapid turnover of stocks is not a good strategy for investors. Typical commissions of 50 to 80 cents a share eat into whatever profits might be made. Keep in mind that professionals might pay 5 cents a share so they have a big advantage at in-and-out trading. In addition, individual investors pay capital gains taxes on any profits. Most professionally managed money is tax-exempt, so that taxes are not a factor in trading decisions.

Those investors who are tempted to time the market should follow any of several longer term strategies that don't predict the short-term ups and downs of the market. These yardsticks have proven to be effective indicators of the current state of the market. They are less useful as short-term trading signals.

- *Dividend-Yield Gauge.* This measure evaluates the stock market's temperature by computing the dividend yield of Standard & Poor's 500-stock Index. This number is calculated by dividing the aggregate per share dividend of the S&P 500 stocks by the S&P 500 Index. Higher dividend yields indicate that cash dividends are high relative to the price of stocks in the index—a signal of undervaluation of stock prices. Lower dividend yields are a sign of overvaluation, since the dividends are low relative to the price of the stocks. Specifically, when the

S&P yield falls below 3 percent, this has historically indicated that the market may be overvalued and investors should be cautious. When the S&P yield rises above 5 percent, a strong buy signal is indicated. In August of 1987 (two months before the crash of 1987), the S&P dividend yield had fallen to 2.5 percent—the lowest in more than 100 years. This ratio is reported weekly in *Barron's* and in Monday's *The Wall Street Journal.*

- *Price-to-Earnings Gauge.* This ratio measures the relationship between the price of common stocks and their annual earnings per share by dividing the price of the common stocks in the S&P 500 Index by the earnings per share of the stocks in the 500 Index. The market is fairly valued when stock prices reflect reasonable expectations regarding earnings growth. When the price-earnings ratio is high, the market is expecting a significant positive future earnings increase—a prediction that may be incorrect. When price-earnings ratios approach historic lows, the market may be too pessimistic about future earnings growth. This ratio is provided weekly in *Barron's* and in Monday's *The Wall Street Journal.* A ratio above 18 often indicates that the market may be ready for a correction. A ratio below 12 usually signals a buying opportunity.
- *Rule of 20.* This measure offers a simple method of evaluating whether the market is vulnerable. According to the rule, when the price-earnings (P/E) ratio of the S&P 500 Index plus the current rate of inflation total 20 or more, investors should watch out. Prior to the October 1987 crash, the rate of inflation was 5 percent and the P/E ratio of the S&P 500 Index was 18.4. The P/E ratio of the Dow Jones is provided in Monday's *The Wall Street Journal* and weekly in *Barron's*.

21

MUTUAL FUNDS

For those investors who lack the time or expertise to manage an investment portfolio, an excellent investment alternative is to purchase shares in mutual funds. A mutual fund is a pool of commingled funds contributed by many investors and managed by a professional fund manager in exchange for a fee. Mutual funds are available to meet a wide range of investment objectives with over 7,000 funds currently serving the needs of investors. These varied needs are being met by the issuance of funds that specialize in municipal bonds, money markets, growth stocks, small company stocks, gold stocks, stocks of firms located in Asia, and other investments.

Advantages of Mutual Funds. Mutual funds offer several advantages that make them extremely attractive vehicles for investors:

1. *Diversification.* A diversified portfolio is very difficult to achieve when funds are limited. A mutual fund offers the investor the opportunity to participate in an investment pool that can contain hundreds of different securities.
2. *Professional Management.* Many investors lack the time or expertise to supervise their investments. Mutual funds are managed by professionals who have the training and experience to make judgments about stock selection and timing.
3. *Liquidity.* Funds can be easily traded. Quotes on the current value of funds are readily available in the financial sections of most newspapers.
4. *Constant Supervising.* Mutual fund managers handle all the details of managing the portfolio. These details include stock transactions, dividends, cash exchanges, rights, and proxy statements. They

arrange for dividend payments and update the performance and tax records for each investor.

Types of Funds. Two basic types of funds exist: closed-end funds and open-end funds. A closed-end fund is an investment company that issues a fixed number of shares. After the shares are issued, the company's shares trade on the stock exchange or over-the-counter. Supply and demand determine share prices, and the share price could be more or less than its intrinsic worth (net asset value). Many of these stock funds trade at a discount to their net asset value for reasons such as exorbitant fees or inferior management. Investors should avoid buying these funds at the initial public offering (IPO). Funds are offered at their actual values and the demand created by the promotional efforts of brokers often pushes them to sell at a premium to net asset value. Once the promotional period ends, prices typically drop to a discount.

Open-end mutual funds, by far the more popular type of mutual fund, are funds that issue or redeem shares at the net asset value (total assets minus total liabilities divided by the number of shares) of the portfolio. Unlike closed-end funds, the number of shares is not fixed but increases as investors purchase more shares. These shares are not traded on any market and are always bought and sold at the net asset value of the portfolio. Typically, large mutual fund organizations manage families of funds that may include, for example, one or more growth funds, gold funds, money market funds, U.S. government securities funds, and small company stock funds. Usually an investor may switch from one fund to another within the same family of funds at no cost or for a small fee.

Mutual funds can also be divided into load and no-load funds. This distinction is based upon whether they charge a sales fee when the fund is initially issued. A sales fee or a commission is known as a "load." A load fund charges a fee of up to 8.5 percent of net asset value that is deducted from the amount of the investment. Thus, a $10,000 purchase of an 8 percent load fund means that $800 is deducted as a fee and only $9,200 is actually invested.

Recently, there has been a trend for mutual funds to reduce their up-front loads (called low-load funds). However, this reduction is often accompanied by increases in yearly fees.

No-load funds are usually purchased directly from the fund without stockbroker involvement. No initial sales charge is deducted from the investment, so $10,000 is actually invested. The performance of load funds has been compared with the performance of no-load funds, and there is no evidence that the former perform better than the latter. An investor interested in short-term profits should unquestionably avoid high load funds.

Fees. Until recently, mutual funds were either load or no-load. But today, fee structures have become more complex and frequently confuse investors. Among these fees are redemption fees, also called contingent deferred sales charges or back-end loads. This fee is charged if an investor's shares are sold, usually within a fixed period. It may be a flat percentage of the sales price or may be based on a sliding scale, say 5 percent the first year, declining in steps to 0 percent in year five.

Under the controversial 12b-1 plans, the fund can charge a fee to pay for its marketing and promotion costs. A 12b-1 fee can be levied on the full value of the investment each year or on the original value of the investment. The maximum fee that can be charged is 0.75 percent.

All funds also charge a management fee in order to compensate the asset managers for their services. These fees range from around 0.3 percent of the fund's assets to 2 percent or more.

Information on fees and other expense data is available on page two of every mutual fund prospectus. You should always read this page before purchasing a mutual fund. Remember that fees reduce your return. You don't always get what you pay for. Thus, the funds that charge the highest fees do not necessarily produce returns justifying those higher costs.

Objectives of Different Funds. Investors can choose from a wide variety of more than 6,000 open-end mutual funds. However, it is extremely important that the objectives of the investor mesh with those of the fund. The Investment Company Act of 1940 requires that mutual funds state their objectives and make this statement available to interested parties. The objectives of a fund are explicitly stated on the second page of the prospectus which every investor should acquire before purchasing a fund. The objective of the fund can only be changed with the agreement of the majority of the shareholders. The following list summarizes the broad objectives of many funds to familiarize investors with the terminology used and its intent:

1. *Money Market Funds* are open-end, no-load funds that invest in money market securities such as treasury bills, negotiable certificates of deposit, and commercial paper. The purpose of these funds is to provide a diversified portfolio of short-term securities to investors who are primarily interested in safety and liquidity. Money market funds are an efficient means for investors with limited resources to invest in securities that have denominations ranging from $10,000 to more than $1 million. Many of these funds require a minimum investment of only $500 and, in addition, provide check-writing privileges against the balance.

2. *Common Stock Funds.* Some funds invest almost exclusively in common stock. Within this category, however, a tremendous difference exists in the type of investment emphasized. Growth funds invest in companies characterized by high rates of growth. These funds seek high rates of return from capital gains and are willing to incur significant risks. Growth and income funds seek to provide both cash dividend income and capital gains. These funds tend to concentrate their investments in large, blue-chip type companies that are less risky. Other funds specialize in small-company stocks. Historically, small-company stocks as a group outperform stocks of larger companies and, of course, carry greater risk. Finally, funds have been introduced that specialize in various areas, for example, certain industries, specific regions, or stock of foreign companies.

3. *Balanced Funds.* These funds contain both common stock and fixed-income securities such as corporate bonds, government bonds, and preferred stock. The combination of these investments is intended to reduce some of the risk associated with fluctuations in the stock market. Due to concern with the preservation of capital, these funds tend to have a conservative investment policy with lower long-term average returns.
4. *Bond Funds.* These funds emphasize high current income and lower risk. However, as is the case for common stock funds, there are a wide variety of bond funds with different investment objectives. Municipal bond funds invest in municipal bonds with tax-exempt income. These bonds are very attractive to investors in high income-tax brackets. Junk bond funds invest in low-quality corporate bonds to earn higher rates of interest income. Many of the bond funds invest in high-grade corporate bonds where the concern is with both safety and income.

Net Asset Value. The net asset value, or NAV, of a mutual fund is the fund's price per share. NAV is calculated after the close of the exchanges each day by taking the closing market value of all securities owned plus all other assets such as cash, subtracting all liabilities, then dividing the result by the total number of shares outstanding.

For money-market funds, the NAV is kept at $1, and $5,000 will buy you 5000 shares. In the case of no-load funds, you pay the NAV when you buy shares. If you invest $10,000 in a no-load fund with an NAV of $20, you will own 500 shares ($10,000 divided by $20). With load funds, that load or sales commission determines the number of shares you buy. For example, if the load is 5 percent, an investment of $5,000 incurs a $250 (.05 times $5,000) sales commission. If the NAV is 25, you would buy 190 shares ($5000 minus $250 divided by $25).

The NAV fluctuates each day as the prices of the securities in the portfolio change. It also changes because of withdrawals to pay fund expenses and distributions to shareholders.

22

INDEX FUNDS

Some of the hottest products in the mutual fund industry are the so-called index funds. More than $400 billion is currently invested in index funds, predominantly by institutional investors. Individual investors have heretofore been a small factor in this market, but recently this has been changing. Unlike most funds that are actively managed to achieve superior returns, index funds don't attempt to time the market or hunt for bargains. They simply try to parallel the investment returns of a specified stock market or bond market index. The investment manager attempts to replicate the results of the target index by holding all or a representative sample of the stocks in the index. Thus, indexing is a passive investment approach which provides broad diversification achieved with low portfolio trading activity.

The theoretical foundation for indexing originated with the formulation of the efficient market hypothesis (EMH). Market efficiency is a description of how prices in a competitive market react to new information. An efficient market is one in which prices adjust rapidly to new information and in which current prices reflect all available information. The adjustment in stock prices occurs so rapidly that an investor cannot use publicly available information to earn above-average profits. Supporters of the EMH state that securities markets are so efficient that it is difficult to outperform the broad market averages through individual stock selection. High portfolio activity to generate superior returns is usually futile because the additional trading costs swallow the returns.

All mutual funds have costs as part of the fund's expense ratio, which includes advisory fees, distribution charges, and operating expenses, and portfolio trading costs, which include brokerage and other costs. The average stock fund has an annual expense ratio of 1.3 percent of investor assets. Further, the typical fund has a portfolio turnover rate of 80 percent per year (buys and sells 80 percent of its portfolio). This turnover generates trading costs of an additional .5 to 1 percent of assets annually. Combining the fund expenses and transaction costs for the typical fund means that about 2 percent of investors' assets are eaten up each year by various costs.

In contrast, one of the significant advantages of an index fund should be its low cost. Advisory fees should be unnecessary, operating expenses low, and transaction costs minimal.

The initial index fund was introduced by Vanguard Group in 1976. The Vanguard Index Trust-500 Portfolio mimics Standard & Poor's (S&P) 500-stock Index and still remains the largest index mutual fund. The S&P Index is composed of large capitalization stocks covering approximately 74 percent of U.S. stock market capitalization (price per share times the number of shares outstanding).

Vanguard's 500 Portfolio operates at an expense ratio of just .20 percent, and transaction costs are less than .10 percent. Its portfolio turnover rate in 1994 was 8 percent, a tenth of a normal stock fund. This $12.2 billion dollar fund served shareholders well in the past decade ending July 1, 1995. Its 14.4 percent annualized return landed the fund in the top 25 percent of all 369 diversified equity funds with ten-year records. Moreover, the fund achieved this record with 14 percent less volatility than the average stock fund.

Index funds are good vehicles for conservative investors who seek a very competitive long-term investment return through broadly diversified portfolios. Index funds won't rank at the top in terms of performance but should also not rank near the bottom. An index fund should provide a very competitive relative performance in the long run.

The Vanguard Group (800-662-7447) has continued to dominate this market by introducing a succession of additional index funds. For those investors who want to track the stock performance of small and medium sized companies, Vanguard introduced The Extended Market Portfolio. This fund mimics the Wilshire 4,500, which is the Wilshire 5,000 index of all U.S. stocks minus the S&P 500 stocks. These stocks trade on the New York Stock Exchange, the American Stock Exchange, and in the NASDAQ over-the-counter (OTC) market.

The low turnover strategy of indexed funds is particularly appropriate where trading costs are high. Thus, many institutional investors use the index approach to invest in small capitalization stocks to minimize the impact of higher trading costs for these investments. The Vanguard Small Capitalization Stock Fund tracks the Russell 2,000 Stock Index, which is the most widely accepted benchmark for small stock index funds. You should expect this index to be more volatile because of its concentration on small companies.

In addition, Vanguard has several international index funds and bond index funds. The international index funds consist of the European Portfolio, the Pacific Portfolio and the Emerging Markets Portfolio. The Vanguard Bond Index Fund tracks the entire spectrum of investment grade U.S. fixed-income instruments. This is an excellent way to participate in the bond market since you are assured participation in a widely diversified portfolio. In addition, with bond funds even more than stock funds, the expense ratio is a critical determinant of how well a fund performs, and the Vanguard Bond Index Fund has the lowest expense ratio in the industry.

23

MONEY MARKET FUNDS

A very safe place to park your savings is in money market mutual funds. Money funds are mutual funds that invest in short-term debt instruments. These include government securities, bank certificates of deposit and commercial paper (short-term corporate IOUs). Commercial paper typically comprises half of a taxable money market fund's portfolio. Because money funds are required by the SEC to invest in debt instruments that mature in an average of 90 days or less, there is relatively little risk of default on those loans.

Although money funds are designed to keep a stable share price of one dollar, the yield will vary as the general level of interest rates changes. Money funds often pay substantially more than a savings or checking account. In addition, you can usually earn 1 to 2 percent more than you would in a bank money-market deposit account.

Although money funds are relatively safe, they are not entirely risk-free. Unlike bank money-market deposit accounts, which are federally insured up to $100,000, money funds are not insured. In the summer of 1990, several major funds suffered defaults on commercial paper they owned. The parent companies purchased the bad commercial paper so that the funds' share value would not drop below one dollar.

These events spurred the SEC and the industry's trade group, the Investment Company Institute (ICI), to back more stringent money-fund safety regulations. Although these investments are not foolproof, no one has lost money through default in a true money fund. Those investors unwilling to assume any credit risk can still buy money funds that invest only in government securities such as Vanguard Money Market Reserves Federal Portfolio (800-662-7447). Although some yield will be sacrificed in return for greater safety, the return will still exceed that of most bank money-market deposit accounts.

Some money funds pay significantly higher yields than others. Although you might assume this difference is caused by the higher-yielding funds putting their investors' money into riskier securities, this may not be the case. The most significant factor causing the difference among funds is the management and operating fees they charge. According to Donoghue's Money Fund Report (800-343-5413), expense charges produce almost two-thirds of the variation in money fund yields.

The average money fund's expense ratio (annual expenses as a percentage of assets) is about 0.75 percent. This ratio indicates that a fund earning 7 percent in interest from its securities would yield a return to its investors of 6.25 percent. Expense charges can vary greatly, ranging from as high as 1.5 percent to as low as about .33 percent at Vanguard. In other words, you could easily boost your return by more than half a percentage point by switching into a fund with lower expenses.

Some funds have temporarily waived their fees altogether in order to attract new business. These special offers help new funds to grow rapidly. Large funds are desirable because fixed operating costs can be spread over a broader shareholder base, and the fund manager's personal return increases because it is typically set as a percentage of assets. You should be aware of when the fee waiver expires. Once the promotion ends, the manager's fee could sharply increase.

Several large money market funds—Vanguard Money Market Reserves Prime (800-662-7447) and Fidelity Cash Reserves (800-544-8888)—have had low expense ratios for many years. As a result, they have consistently been among the higher-yielding money market funds.

The dividends you earn on most money market funds is fully taxable. Investors in a high tax bracket might find tax-exempt money funds attractive. Like all money funds they invest in, short-term debt securities, and their share prices remain at one dollar. But tax-free funds buy only municipal securities, which are generally exempt from federal tax and sometimes, state and local taxes.

Before investing in a tax-free money fund, you should calculate the taxable equivalent yield. This process involves two steps:

Step 1: Subtract your tax bracket from 1. Assuming you're in the 28 percent tax bracket, the answer would be .72.

Step 2: Divide the tax-free yield by the answer you got in Step 1, .72. If the tax-free yield is 6 percent, divide 6 percent by .72. The answer, 8.33 percent, is the taxable equivalent yield.

Some tax-free choices for investors in the higher tax brackets include:

Dreyfus Tax-Exempt Money Fund (800-645-6561)
Strong Municipal (800-368-3863)
Calvert Tax-Free Reserves (800-368-2748)

If you live in a state with high income taxes, you can further reduce taxes by investing in single-state tax-free funds. These funds let you skip state as well as federal taxes by investing only in securities issued by municipalities in one state. Most states exempt their residents from state income tax on municipal securities issued in that state. Therefore, the interest from single-state funds is free of state taxes as well as federal taxes for residents of that state. Moreover, if you live in a county or city that has an income tax, the interest is generally exempt from their local taxes.

Assets in this sector of the mutual fund industry have mushroomed recently. Both *Barron's* and *The Wall Street Journal* list these funds. Among the prominent ones are:

Calvert Tax-Free California Portfolio (800-368-2748)
Nuveen Massachusetts Tax-Free Money Fund (800-621-7227)
Dreyfus New Jersey Tax-Exempt Money Market (800-648-9048)
T. Rowe Price New York Tax-Free Money Funds (800-638-5660)

24

MUTUAL FUND PROSPECTUS

The prospectus is the single most important document produced by a mutual fund, and every investor should examine a prospectus before buying a mutual fund. Before a fund will accept your initial order, you must acknowledge that you are familiar with the prospectus. Current shareholders must receive new prospectuses when updated (at least once every 14 months).

The prospectus is organized into sections, and it must cover certain specific topics. The descriptions can seem very technical, but there is good reason for this precision. The prospectus is an official document that requires SEC approval. The SEC has strict guidelines on what can be said in a prospectus and how information must be presented on past performance, expenses, and fees. Remember, the SEC's approval of a prospectus does not imply approval of any investment.

The cover of the prospectus usually gives a quick rundown of the fund including its investment objectives, sales or redemption charges, minimum investment, retirement plans available, address and phone number. The body of the prospectus provides a more detailed description.

Near the front of the prospectus is a table that describes all the expenses and fees. The table includes three sections. The first section describes maximum sales charges on purchases and reinvested dividends, deferred sales charges, redemption fees, and exchange fees.

Until the mid-1980s, mutual funds were split between the "loads" (which could charge up to 8.5 percent) and the no-loads. A load is a sales commission that goes to whomever sells fund shares to an investor and does not go to anyone responsible for managing the fund's assets. If you invest $1,000 and pay a 5 percent load, only $950 of your money gets invested. If you purchased a no-load fund, the entire $1,000 is invested for you.

More recently, mutual fund companies have introduced a variety of fees and charges such as "contingent deferred sales charges" and 12b-1 fees. Contingent deferred sales charges are often called "redemption fees," "exit fees," or "back-end loads." To illustrate, a fund might charge you 5 percent of its value if sold within the first year. Each year thereafter your exit fee might drop by 1 percent. After six years, no redemption fee is charged.

The controversial 12b-1 charge, named for the SEC rule which allows funds to levy it, is meant to help defray marketing and distribution costs. Instead of paying this charge once when you buy the fund (front-end load), or when you sell it (back-end load), you pay this fee annually based upon the total net asset value of the mutual fund. Funds with 12b-1 plans can charge up to a maximum of 0.75 percent of assets per year, or $.75 per $100 of assets.

The second section of the table describes the annual operating expenses, expressed as a percentage of fund net asset value. These expenses include management fees, 12b-1 fees, and other expenses. All funds charge annual management fees which generally range from .5 to 1.5 percent of net assets. Beginning in May 1988, the SEC required mutual fund companies to show in a table how fees would affect a hypothetical $1,000 investment, assuming a 5 percent annual rate of return. This section also indicates the total dollar cost if the investor's shares were to be redeemed at the end of one year, three years, five years, and ten years.

There is no evidence that funds with higher charges deliver better performance than those with reduced fees. Although the expense ratio is not the only thing to consider in buying a fund, it should certainly be a factor. Certainly, an expense ratio over 2 percent is excessive (the average for stock funds is about 1.3 percent). The average bond fund charges 0.95 percent. Expense ratios are particularly important in selecting bond funds. A good stock fund manager may be able to overcome a high management fee. It is very difficult for bond fund managers to overcome a steep management fee because bonds generally don't soar the way stocks do.

One of the most important sections of the prospectus is the section containing condensed financial information, which provides statistics on per share income and capital changes. The per-share figures are shown for the life of the fund or ten years, whichever is less.

The per-share section summarizes fund financial activities over its fiscal year. The financial changes summarized include increases in net asset value due to dividend and interest payments received, and capital gains from investment activity. Decreases in net asset value are caused by capital losses from investment activity, investment expenses, and payouts to fund shareholders in the form of distributions.

The last line in the per-share section will be the net asset value at the end of the year. The net asset value is calculated by dividing the total assets of the fund by the number of mutual shares outstanding.

The financial ratios at the bottom of the table are important indicators of fund strategy and performance. The expense ratio is shown in the fund expenses section of the prospectus. The ratio of net investment income to average net assets is similar to dividend yield for a stock and reflects the investment objective of the fund. Bond funds would typically have ratios that are more than twice those of stock funds.

The portfolio turnover rate is calculated by dividing the lower of purchases or sales by average net assets. It tells you how frequently securities are bought and sold by a fund. The higher the turnover, the greater the brokerage costs incurred by the fund. A 100 percent turnover rate means that securities in the portfolio have been held for an average of one year, and a 50 percent turnover indicates that securities have been held for an average of two years. The average portfolio turnover rate for a mutual fund is about 80 percent.

Check to see if the portfolio turnover rate is consistent with the objective of the fund. Aggressive growth mutual funds will typically have higher portfolio turnover rates while conservative funds will have lower portfolio turnover rates. In addition, you would like to see a fairly consistent turnover rate over time. A consistent turnover rate is an indication that the portfolio manager is adhering to the investment objective of the fund.

The investment objective section of the prospectus describes the types of investments the fund will make and the amount, in percentage, of assets the fund will normally invest in certain types of investments. This section will indicate whether the fund is seeking capital appreciation or income. It will often include the investment philosophy of the portfolio manager, a description of how the securities are selected, and the anticipated level of portfolio turnover.

The fund management section names the investment advisor and provides a schedule of compensation for the advisor. Most advisors are paid based on a sliding scale that decreases as assets under management increase. If you want additional information about a fund's officers and directors, including a short biography, you can request what is called a statement of additional information from the mutual fund company. It provides details not included in your prospectus such as the names, occupations, and compensation of directors and officers.

Surprisingly, most prospectuses do not include the name of the portfolio manager. To get this information quickly, place a telephone call to the fund. It is also a good idea to ask how long the portfolio manager has been in that position. Increasingly, portfolio managers are moving from fund to fund, and in these instances, the track record earned by the fund's previous manager is irrelevant. Investors should not only check a fund's performance but also make certain that the manager who earned the record is still there.

Profile Prospectus. On August 1, 1995, eight fund companies—Fidelity, Vanguard, T. Rowe Price, IDS, Pacific Horizon, Capital Research and Management,

Dreyfus, and Scudder—began testing what is called a profile prospective, a two-page abbreviated document that is a summarized and simplified version of the fund prospectus. Initially, profiles will be available for a stock, bond, and money-market fund from each of the eight companies working with regulators on the project.

Although the traditional prospectus will be distributed along with the profiles, the hope is that the streamlined documents will be able to stand on their own. A survey will be conducted by the SEC and fund companies to determine whether the documents contain enough information for an investor to make an intelligent decision.

The profiles will describe a fund's objectives, investment strategies, risks, expenses, and past performance in just two pages. A typical prospectus can take 50 pages to give the same information.

Only new investors at the eight fund groups will get profile prospectuses. If the profiles are found to provide adequate disclosures and are approved for all funds, they could significantly change how funds are bought and sold. The documents will be tested for a one-year period.

25

MUTUAL FUND SELECTION

This book advocates buying mutual funds as an effective way to build wealth and prepare for retirement. Mutual fund investing is easy and these funds are very closely regulated so there is little chance of fraud. Mutual funds pool money from thousands of investors. As one of those investors, you are buying into a professionally managed, diversified portfolio of stocks, bonds, money-market securities, or a mixture of all three.

You can generally buy or sell a mutual fund at any time. The attractiveness of this type of investment is evidenced by the fact that one family in three has a mutual fund account. The total amount invested exceeds $3 trillion, a 24-fold increase since 1980.

With more than 7,000 mutual funds to choose from, many beginning investors want an answer to the question: "How do I decide which one to pick?" The answer is easy if you are willing to do a little homework.

If you have limited capital and can only afford to buy a single mutual fund, a balanced fund, which divides its assets between stocks and bonds, is a good choice. The proportion of stocks and bonds that will be held is usually stated in the investment objective (page two of the prospectus), but it may vary over time. Balanced funds are generally less volatile than stock funds and provide a relatively high dividend yield.

Balanced funds offer you diversification by having your money invested for growth (stocks) and income (bonds). These funds are less volatile or risky than most stock funds because the inclusion of bonds reduces the impact of a bear market on the returns of the portfolio.

As a result, these funds represent a good compromise between pure bond funds, which provide lower returns with less risk, and stock funds, which generally produce higher returns at greater risk.

Although many business periodicals and newspapers cover mutual funds, one source is particularly useful to mutual fund investors. Each fall (usually in the late August issue) *Forbes* evaluates mutual funds and makes recommendations. This issue should be consulted by all investors agonizing over which mutual fund to buy.

The *Forbes* survey provides an Honor Roll of 20 funds that demonstrate consistency of results and strength in bear markets. In addition, *Forbes* provides a list of Best Buys that looks at cost, risk, and return. Among the Best Buys listed in the *Forbes* August 28, 1995 issue are the following balanced funds:

- Vanguard Wellesley Income Fund (800-662-7447)
- Fidelity Asset Manager (800-544-8888)
- Vanguard Wellington Fund (800-662-7447)
- Dodge & Cox Balanced Fund (800-621-3979)
- T. Rowe Price Balanced Fund (800-638-5660)

The returns on these funds ranged from 10.7 percent to 12.2 percent over the previous five years, according to *Forbes.* Incidentally, all of these funds are no-load funds, which means that no initial sales charge is deducted from the amount you invest.

Once your investment capital exceeds $10,000, you should start thinking about how to combine different types of funds in a mutual fund portfolio. Funds are by nature diverse because they invest in many securities. Putting your money in a variety of them contributes to the diversification of your portfolio by smoothing out the market ups and downs. How you put together a fund portfolio depends a great deal on your personal circumstances, including your age, your ability to tolerate risk, and your need for income. But whatever your situation, it's wise to have a substantial investment in the stock market. This recommendation applies even to people who are 65 years of age. They can expect to live long enough for taxes and inflation to drastically cut the purchasing power of fixed income investments.

Ken Gregory, editor of the *No-Load Fund Analyst* (800-776-9555), recommends that conservative investors who can tolerate an occasional year when portfolio losses are as high as 5 percent structure a portfolio of about one-third stocks and two-thirds bonds. If you can tolerate a rare year when losses exceed 10 percent, he recommends a stock allocation as high as 70 percent.

Once you have determined your asset mix, what types of stock funds should you select for your stock portfolio? There is no simple answer to this question. Most analysts recommend owning a growth fund and a "value" fund because these two investment styles tend to do well at different times. Growth-stock managers search for companies with rapid earnings growth and value managers purchase stocks that are cheap (relative to earnings and assets).

In addition, you should consider buying a small-company stock fund and a fund that specializes in foreign stocks. As part of a total portfolio, foreign stocks help to lower risk, because they don't always move in patterns similar to U.S. stocks. In addition, many foreign economies have higher growth rates than U.S. economies; some have significantly outperformed U.S. stocks.

Appropriately diversifying your choices of mutual funds should provide a return at least equal to that of the Standard & Poor's 500 with significantly less risk. Again, use *Forbes* to assist you in picking the best funds.

In choosing bonds, pay close attention to the fees charged. Bond-fund managers have more difficulty in producing returns that justify higher fees than do stock-fund managers. You should select no-load funds that charge minimum annual fees. The Vanguard bond funds (800-662-7447) are excellent choices because Vanguard has almost made a religion of charging the lowest fees. Municipal bonds remain attractive for those investors in the 28 percent or higher tax bracket seeking interest income that is exempt from federal taxation. Specific fund choices are highlighted in the "Best Buys" section of *Forbes*.

26

UNIT INVESTMENT TRUSTS

Unit investment trusts (UITs) are fixed, closed-end portfolios in which investors can purchase units of participation for as little as $1,000. They are fixed in the sense that the entire portfolio is accumulated at its beginning before sales to the public start. Closed-end means that there are a limited number of units for sale.

A UIT's portfolio remains the same except in a few circumstances, such as when a bond is called. Although the vast majority of UITs are in bonds, some trusts in recent years have been formed around a variety of investment concepts, such as those that emulate stock indexes such as the S&P 500. Each type of trust is composed of one category of securities such as municipal bonds, certificates of deposit, utility common stocks, or corporate bonds. A unit represents functional ownership of all securities in the fund and entitles the owner to a proportionate share of the income produced by those securities. Interest or dividend income is usually distributed on a monthly basis. The principal is returned when the securities mature or are redeemed or sold, unless the investor sells the units before that time.

UITs are not managed, so there is little or no management fee. Since the portfolio is fixed, you know exactly what you own. The portfolio remains unchanged with few exceptions. All UITs have fixed lives, varying from a few months to 30 years. At maturity, the bonds are sold and investors receive the proceeds.

UITs are aimed at the small investor who can't afford to diversify because of the large minimum investment in individual bonds. Investors should plan to purchase UITs as long-term investments. Liquidity, if there is any, is limited by provisions in the contract. While UITs offer diversity and professional selection, they carry high sales fees. The sales charges of 2 to 5 percent reduce their value as a short-term investment. If you expect to sell in fewer than eight years, a managed no-load mutual fund is preferable.

Investors should understand the fee structure and sales charges. The charges are usually up front with no fees or penalties if sold before maturity. Determine if the broker or other selling agent maintains a secondary or resale market so that the units can be redeemed before maturity.

Remember that if interest rates climb, the value of a bond UIT goes down. On the other hand, if interest rates drop, your trust will appreciate.

Defaults and bond calls can significantly reduce the anticipated return of a unit investment trust. For example, a portfolio might include bonds bought at a price of $115 but if these bonds are called (redeemed before maturity) at a price of $100, there will be a capital loss and the yield will drop. Similarly, zero-coupon bonds called before maturity and while still priced at a deep discount can significantly reduce expected yield.

Investors concerned about the possibility of default can choose an insured trust, where either the underlying bonds or the specific portfolio are insured by a private company. More than half of current UITs are so insured. But although the insurance provides protection against defaults, there is no protection against calls except to evaluate this risk before buying and be aware of the danger.

Sponsors of UITs are brokerage firms. Traditionally, the two largest sponsors have been Merrill Lynch and John Nuveen & Company, although other brokerage firms have entered this market. Investors should not purchase a UIT only on the basis of advertised current return (the annual interest earnings divided by the offering price). Trusts can boost this current return by purchasing junk (high-risk, high-yield) bonds. Conservative investors should only select UITs composed of investment grade bonds.

27

FOREIGN SECURITIES

As the world economy becomes increasingly interdependent, many investors are now becoming aware of the profits to be made by investing in foreign securities. With 50 percent of the world's publicly traded stocks registered outside the United States, opportunities abound for the investor willing to expend the time and effort to analyze those markets. Returns on U.S. stock have lagged behind many of these markets since 1960.

An investment in a foreign stock can lead to a profit or loss in two ways:

1. The price of the stock in its local currency can go up or down.
2. The value of the foreign currency relative to the U.S. dollar may rise or fall.

The optimal situation is to have the price of the stock rise in the local currency and the value of the foreign currency rise against the U.S. dollar. The weakness of the U.S. dollar in the 1990s enhanced the profits made by investment in foreign stock.

Of the several methods for investing in foreign stock, the two most popular for individual investors are American Depository Receipts (ADRs) and mutual funds.

American Depository Receipts (ADRs). Individuals who wish to purchase specific foreign securities should purchase ADRs. ADRs are negotiable receipts representing ownership of stock in a foreign corporation traded on an exchange or in the over-the-counter market. ADRs are issued only on widely held and actively traded corporations. Furthermore, they are very liquid and have transaction costs comparable to U.S. stock. They are issued by an American bank and represent shares on deposit with the American bank's foreign office or custodian. ADRs allow investors to buy or sell foreign securities without actually taking possession of them. Purchase is made and dividends are received in U.S. dollars. Approximately 1,400 foreign corporations have ADRs listed against their securities with the great majority traded in the over-the-counter market. In 1994, ADRs accounted for 6.3 percent of the dollar volume on U.S. stock exchanges, a gain of 50 percent from 1990.

Mutual Funds. The easiest and safest way to invest in foreign securities is to buy one of the mutual funds that confines its investments to foreign securities. This course would be preferable for those investors who lack the time or inclination to investigate this market. International stock funds offer the advantage of participation in a diversified portfolio of foreign stocks as well as professional management.

International stock funds were sterling performers in the 1980s. The run-up in foreign stock prices (and Japanese markets in particular) made these funds some of the top performers of that decade. However, even if this performance is unlikely to be duplicated, investing a portion of your assets in international stock funds does make sense. Many countries have experienced and will continue to experience higher economic growth rates than the United States.

Four excellent no-load choices include T. Rowe Price International Stock (800-638-5660), Scudder International Fund (800-225-2470), Vanguard International Equity European (800-662-7447) and Vanguard International Equity Pacific (800-662-7447). Prior to purchasing any international stock funds, you should obtain a copy of the prospectus. A prospectus will describe the investment philosophy of the fund.

More than 140 closed-end funds specialize in stocks of individual countries. Unlike open-end funds, closed-end funds issue a fixed number of shares that trade on an exchange or over the counter. Their prices move up or down in response to investor demand just like common stocks. The fluctuation of their prices means that the price is often above or below net asset value (NAV), the value of the stocks in the portfolio divided by the number of shares. When the price of a fund is above NAV, its price trades at a "premium"; below NAV, it trades at a "discount." Although closed-end shares may trade at a premium to NAV for a short period after their initial offering, they generally trade at a discount to NAV. In bear (declining) markets they trade at a greater discount; when the market turns bullish, the discount declines.

Closed-end fund prices tend to be volatile, and these funds should be avoided by conservative investors. If you are interested, however, purchases should only be made when the discount widens. The amount of discount or premium on closed-end funds is published weekly in *Barron's* (800-228-6262).

Global Funds. Every investor should give serious consideration to the global diversification of his or her investment portfolio. After World War II, the capitalization (number of shares times price per share) of the U.S. stock market comprised 90 percent of the world total. Currently, the U.S. share is down to a third and it is expected to continue to drop in the future.

Investors should take advantage of opportunities to participate in the faster growth of many foreign economies by investing internationally. Although there is no magic formula for determining the optimum allocation, anywhere from 10 to 25 percent of the portfolio is a reasonable allocation for conservative investors.

Funds that invest in non-U.S. securities are generally called international funds. International funds include only non-U.S. securities such as those from countries like Japan, France, and Korea. The more recently introduced global funds hold both U.S. and non-U.S. securities. They can invest anywhere in the world, including in the United States. Globals should outperform pure internationals when the U.S. market is especially strong, while internationals should excel when foreign stock markets are booming. Interested investors can consider Scudder Global (800-225-2470), Janus Worldwide (800-525-3713), or Tweedy Browne Global Value (800-432-4789).

28

CORPORATE BONDS

One of the most important financing tools for corporations is the issuance of corporate bonds. Bonds are long-term debt obligations that are secured by specified assets or, in the case of an unsecured bond, which is called a debenture, they rely only on a promise to repay the debt. In effect, a bond investor has lent money to the bond issuer. In return, the issuer of that bond promises to pay interest and to repay the principal at maturity. A bond's "maturity," or the length of time until the principal is scheduled to repaid, can vary from five to 40 years.

Investors have greater assurance of receiving interest on bonds than dividends on most common stock because bondholders are creditors of the issuing corporation. As creditors, bonds have a prior claim on earnings and assets ranking ahead of preferred and common stockholders (i.e., interest must be paid to the bondholders before dividends can be distributed to stockholders). In case of dissolution or bankruptcy, bondholders have a prior claim on assets over stockholders. Only corporations in extreme financial difficulty will fail to pay the interest on their bonds.

Bond Characteristics. Investment in a corporate bond is the purchase of the corporation's promise to pay interest and to repay the principal at a specified maturity date. Bonds are typically issued in denominations of $1,000, called the face, par, or maturity value. If an investor buys five bonds, the total face value or par value is $5,000, which means that the corporation will repay $5,000 when the bonds mature. In addition, the corporation promises to pay periodic interest at a specified rate on the face value. The interest rate is commonly called the coupon or stated rate, and payments are usually made semiannually—although the interest rate is generally expressed as an annual rate.

The price of a bond is determined by such factors as the interest rate stated on the bond (coupon rate), the length of its term to maturity, credit quality of the bond, and the general level of interest rates. Bonds fluctuate in price, and market value is largely determined by changes in interest rates. As the general level of interest rates rises, bond prices go down to keep yields in line with market levels; as the general level of interest rates declines, bond prices increase.

A critical factor in determining the interest rate a bond must pay to attract investors is the credit quality of the bond. Corporate bonds are assigned to different risk classifications by several rating agencies that indicate the default risk associated with the purchase of securities. The two most important companies evaluating bonds, Moody's Investors Service and Standard & Poor's, generally give similar bond ratings. Exhibit I provides the risk classifications and a general description of their meaning. Bonds rated AAA by Standard & Poor's or Aaa by Moody's are the highest-grade obligations, meaning they possess the ultimate degree of protection as to principal and interest. Bonds rated below BBB or Baa are speculative in nature and are called high-yield or (pejoratively) junk bonds. These lower-quality bonds must pay higher yields in order to attract investors. The risk of a bond defaulting is less than the risk that its rating will be downgraded, a development that will cause a sudden reduction in market value.

Bond prices are quoted as a percentage of face value. For example, a closing price of 97⅞ means that the actual price of the bond is 97⅞ × $1,000 par value = $978.75 for each bond. In a discussion of bonds, the term "basis point" is often used. A basis point is 1/100th of 1 percent and is a convenient way to discuss changes in yields. For example, an increase in yield from 7 percent to 7.5 percent is a 50-basis point increase.

Bond Yields. Understanding the different definitions of yield is critical to understanding bond pricing. Coupon yield is the interest rate stated on the bond. A coupon yield of 10 percent indicates that a bond with a face value of $1,000 will pay $100 interest. Current yield is obtained by dividing the coupon rate by the latest price. The current yield is higher than the coupon yield if the bond was purchased at a discount and is lower if purchased at a premium. The yield to maturity is the most important concept of yield because it is the yield upon which all bond prices are based. The current yield only measures today's return, but the yield to maturity measures the rate of return when the bond is held to maturity. It includes both interest and the appreciation to face value at maturity when the bonds are bought at a discount or depreciation to face value when the bonds are bought at a premium.

EXHIBIT 1
Bond Ratings

Description	Moody's	Standard & Poor's
High Grade	Aaa	AAA
	Aa	AA
Medium Grade	A	A
	Baa	BBB
Speculative	Ba	BB
	B	B
Default	Caa	CCC
	Ca	CC
	C	C

Why Buy Bonds? Corporate bonds can be excellent investments for those investors interested in protecting their principal and receiving a steady stream of income. Corporate bond interest will exceed the income to be received from government bonds, CDs, money market funds, or stocks. Bonds are particularly appropriate for tax-protected retirement plans in which interest can compound free of tax.

Most corporate bonds are sold with a "call" feature that allows the issuer to redeem the bond prior to its maturity. Companies often call in bonds when general interest rates are several percentage points lower than the coupon rate on the bond. When this happens, bondholders are forced to reinvest the funds at lower interest rates.

Investors need to be aware of the call features of the bonds they acquire. Call features are not specified in the financial section of the newspaper. However, this information does appear in Standard & Poor's *Bond Guide* (212-208-8000) available at your library, on the back of bond certificates, and in bond prospectuses. To protect yourself against a call, you can purchase newly issued bonds or recently issued bonds. These bonds often cannot be called for five or ten years.

Stick with those corporate bonds with high bond ratings. These include the giant corporations such as General Motors, IBM, Exxon, General Electric, and AT&T. Unlike treasury securities, which have no credit risk, corporate bonds are only as strong as the issuer or guarantor. Your investment is protected by the financial strength of the corporation. High quality bonds will pay lower interest rates because safety is traded off for lower yields. Don't chase higher yields by buying speculative bonds. You'll sleep better if your bonds are rated at least A.

An excellent way to invest in corporate bonds is to buy no-load mutual funds that invest primarily in corporate bonds. Shares can be purchased for as little as $500, with smaller additional investments accepted thereafter. The yields may be slightly less than direct investments in corporate bonds, but you get the benefit of diversification, professional management, and convenience. Two excellent no-load choices are Vanguard Intermediate-Term Corporate (800-662-7447) and Vanguard Short-Term Corporate (800-662-7447).

You should be aware of several pitfalls in bond investments. First, corporate bond interest is subject to federal, state, and local taxes. In contrast, treasury securities are exempt from state and local taxes, and municipal bonds are exempt from federal income tax and state and local taxes in the area where issued. Make sure you compute the after-tax yield when you compare the returns of the various types of bonds.

29

MUNICIPAL BONDS

Municipal bonds (tax-exempt bonds) are debt securities issued by state and local governments and local government agencies and authorities. These bonds are issued for a variety of reasons, such as the financing of temporary shortfalls in revenues or the financing of the construction of hospitals, bridges, and sports stadiums. Municipal bonds differ from corporate bonds in three significant respects:

1. The interest on municipal bonds is exempt from federal income taxes. In addition, if these bonds are issued in the investor's state of residency, they are also exempt from state and local income taxes. This tax-exempt feature is what makes municipal bonds or "munis" so attractive to investors in higher income tax brackets. Without the tax-exemption, many municipalities would have a difficult time marketing their debt securities.

   For example, consider an investor in the 30 percent income tax bracket who is choosing between a municipal bond and a corporate bond. Assume the bonds are of equivalent risk, but the muni pays a coupon rate of 6 percent and the corporate bond pays 8 percent. The following formula can be used to compare the two investments:

[before-tax interest] × [1 – investor's tax rate] = [after-tax interest rate]

| 8% | × | 70% | = | 5.6% |

   The 8 percent interest on the corporate bond is equivalent to 5.6 percent after tax. This formula reveals that 30 percent of the interest income goes to pay for taxes while the investor retains 70 percent. Clearly, at 6 percent, the muni pays greater after-tax interest.

2. Most municipal bond issues are serial bond issues as opposed to the term maturities of corporate bonds. A serial bond issue involves a series of maturity dates. The advantage of having a portion of the bonds mature periodically over the life of the issue is that it spreads fixed principal repayment obligations over a number of years to correspond to the flow of tax revenue receipts. In contrast, corporate bonds typically have a single maturity date such as ten or 20 years.
3. Most municipal bonds are issued in $5,000 denominations, and corporate bonds are issued in $1,000 denominations. Their prices are seldom quoted in the daily press. An investor interested in obtaining specific quotes can contact municipal bond dealers or refer to a publication such as *The Blue List.*

Types of Municipal Bond Issues. Two general types of munis exist: general obligation bonds and revenue bonds. General obligation bonds (GOs) are backed by a pledge of a governmental unit's full faith and credit for the prompt repayment of both principal and interest. Since they are backed by the full taxing power of the issuer, they are considered the safest munis. Default risk has been very low, although the recent bankruptcy of Orange County in California might make it seem otherwise. Even when default has occurred in the past, most issuers have repaid the entire principal.

Interest rate risk is greater than default risk for the majority of GOs. As general interest rates rise, the price of munis goes down. Bonds with longer maturities and/or lower coupon rates (interest rate stated on the bond) are most affected by changes in interest rates.

Revenue bonds are payable from the revenues generated by a particular project such as a sewer, gas or electric system, airport, or toll bridge financed by the issue. If the bond is issued to finance the construction of one of these enterprises, the revenues produced by these enterprises are pledged to pay interest and repay the principal. Revenue bonds generally possess higher default risk than

GOs and, as a consequence, must usually pay higher interest rates to attract investors.

Rating Municipal Bonds. Standard & Poor's Corporation and Moody's Investors Service are the two major municipal rating agencies. Although other factors in addition to a bond's rating affect the price of a bond, ratings clearly have a significant effect on a bond's price. The higher the rating, the lower the interest cost and conversely the lower the rating, the higher the interest cost. The symbols used by Moody's and Standard & Poor's are the same symbols used in rating corporate bonds. Moody's ratings are in descending order of quality: Aaa, Aa, A, Baa, Ba, B, Caa, Ca, and C. Standard & Poor's ratings are in descending order of quality: AAA, AA, A, BBB, BB, B, CCC, CC, C, and D. Investment grade is indicated for those bonds with ratings equal to or greater than Baa for Moody's and BBB for Standard & Poor's. Bonds rated below those categories are generally designated as "speculative." Conservative investors should only buy munis with at least an A rating. The additional risk associated with lower-quality bonds is not justified by the slightly higher yields.

One of the unusual aspects of the municipal bond market is that munis can be insured through underwriters such as American Municipal Bond Assurance Corporation (AMBAC) and Municipal Bond Insurance Association (MBIA). For a premium of .1 to 2 percent of total principal and interest paid by the issuer, the insurer will pay the principal and interest on the bond should the issuer default. Typically, these bonds pay lower yields than uninsured bonds with similar features. An insured bond is given an AAA rating by Standard & Poor's. It should be noted that insurance does not protect against interest rate risk.

For those investors with limited time and resources, the best way to invest in munis is to purchase municipal bond mutual funds. This approach affords the investor diversification as well as constant supervision by professional management. The minimum required investment is usually $1,000. Three excellent choices are: Fidelity

Municipal Bond (800-544-8888), Scudder Managed Municipal (800-225-2470), and Vanguard Long-Term Municipal (800-662-7447).

If you live in a high-tax state, munis issued by your state and local governments can exempt you from state and local taxes. This advantage can increase your yield by as much as 1 to 1.5 percent. Some examples of single state municipal bond funds include Putnam New York (800-2251581) and MFS Managed California (800-225-2606).

Insured Bonds. In December 1994, the muni market was startled when Orange County disclosed it had what was eventually determined to be about $2 billion in losses in its investment portfolio. Within days, the county filed for bankruptcy, which put all debt service in doubt and precipitated a plunge in bond prices. Although historically munis have been among the safest bets for conservative, yield-conscious investors, the headlines were not reassuring. What should conservative investors do?

One alternative for those venturesome enough to buy individual issues is to buy insured munis. Insured munis now comprise about 30 percent of the market and trade about one to one and a half percentage points below comparable uninsured issues. Munis insured by all the major bond insurers qualify for AAA ratings. Don't assume, however, that insured munis carry no risk. The guarantees of the bond insurers are largely untested and some are stronger than others. Even munis backed by AAA-rated insurance companies can default.

The safest bet for the conservative investor is to buy municipal bond funds that buy munis with bond ratings of no less than "A." The Fidelity, Vanguard, and Scudder funds contain hundreds of issues. The bankruptcy of one or several issues would not have a serious impact on the entire portfolio of these funds.

30

ZERO COUPON BONDS

Zero coupon bonds—also referred to as zeros—are so named because they do not pay cash interest. Instead, the obligations are sold to you at a deep discount from their face amount over the years. In other words, these bonds are "stripped" of their interest coupons, and this interest is added to the principal every six months. When zeros mature, you get this interest back in a balloon payment. You buy zero coupon bonds at a small fraction of their $1,000 face amount, then redeem them at full value at maturity.

Zeros are a good investment if you know you will be needing a lump sum of money at a certain date in the future. Zeros are suitable investments for Individual Retirement Accounts (IRAs) and other tax-deferred or tax-free accounts. The Internal Revenue Service requires taxable holders to declare annually as income a prorated portion of the dollar difference between the purchase price and the maturity value of zeros. When zeros are held in IRAs, however, taxes are not due until the money is withdrawn. Zeros are often used, as well, in planning for specific investment goals, including funding anticipated college tuition payments.

A wide range of maturities and types of zeros are available. Because there are so many maturity dates to pick from, you can select the maturity that matches the time you'll need the money and know precisely how much you'll have on that date. Simply determine the maturity you need—the longer the maturity, the greater the multiplier effect:

Year you need $50,000	Number of bonds you need	Price per bond	Total purchase price	Yield to maturity	Amount at maturity
5 years (2001)	50	$633	$31,650	8.00%	$50,000
10 years (2006)	50	$419	$20,950	8.20%	$50,000
20 years (2016)	50	$191	$9,500	8.12%	$50,000

Zero coupon U.S. Treasury securities are particularly popular with investors. Such obligations are available in maturities ranging from a few months to about 30 years. All U.S. Treasury securities are direct obligations of the U.S. government, which means that they're backed by the full faith and credit of the U.S. government. When held to maturity, treasury securities guarantee both your principal and interest. In addition, interest from treasuries is exempt from both state and local taxes.

Zero coupon treasury receipts were introduced by Merrill Lynch in 1982. The success of Merrill Lynch's Treasury Investment Growth Receipts—known on Wall Street as TIGRs—led a number of other brokerage houses to market similar products. Those instruments are being packaged under various other appellations, of which CATS is perhaps best known.

CATS—Certificates of Accrual on Treasury Securities—are marketed by Salomon Brothers and a group of other brokerage houses. Some CATS are listed on the New York Stock Exchange, and trading information on them can be found in the financial pages of many newspapers under the heading "New York Exchange Bonds."

During 1985, the U.S. Treasury established a zero coupon program known as STRIPS (Separate Trading of Registered Interest and Principal of Securities). Under this program, banks, savings and loans, and similar institutions that maintain book entry accounts at a Federal Reserve Bank can have selected treasury issues separated into their component parts (principal and interest). The institutions buy treasury bonds, then offer to the public safekeeping certificates for zeros in maturity denominations of $1,000. STRIPS offer a range of 120 maturities at three-month intervals covering a period of one to 30 years. Treasury STRIPS must be purchased from a stockbroker.

In May 1988, zero-coupon securities became available that are derived from bonds issued by a federally sponsored agency, the Financing Corporation (FICO). FICO was created by Congress to raise money for the ailing Federal Savings & Loan Insurance Corp. The principal of these bonds is secured by U.S. Treasury securities that match the maturities on FICO bonds. The FICO zeros provide both high quality and greater yields than zeros derived from treasury bonds.

Zeros, like straight bonds, rise in price when interest rates fall and fall when rates rise. The lack of interest payments to dampen market swings makes zeros more volatile in price than other bonds. If interest rates rise, prices of zeros can fall dramatically. Investors purchasing zeros should intend to hold them to maturity.

For small investors, investing in zeros through the purchase of mutual funds makes sense because they require only a $1,000 minimum investment. In order to obtain competitive interest rates, investors buying zeros directly would have to spend at least $4,500 to $5,000 that would buy a zero with a face value of $10,000.

Two big fund companies have set up mutual funds to capitalize on the popularity of zeros. The biggest forces in the market are the Benham Capital Management Group (800-227-8380); (800-982-6150 in California) and Scudder, Stevens & Clark (800-225-2470). The Benham and Scudder funds are portfolios of zero coupon U.S. Treasury securities that mature in five-year increments.

31

GINNIE MAES

The Government National Mortgage Association (GNMA or Ginnie Mae) was established by Congress in 1968 to attract new funds into the housing market by appealing to a broader spectrum of the investment community than traditional mortgage investors. GNMA securities represent pools of mortgages that are backed by the full faith and credit of the U.S. government. GNMA has full authority to borrow without limitation from the U.S. Treasury to meet its obligations under various mortgage-backed securities guarantee agreements.

GNMA does not buy the mortgages to be pooled. Rather, GNMA guarantees timely payment of interest and principal and provides a liquid security that can be easily traded. The mortgages to be pooled are held by a custodian, usually the trust department of a bank or a mortgage banker. If a pooled mortgage goes into default, the issuer advances payments that are then repaid by GNMA.

Ginnie Maes will typically yield about .5 to 1.0 percent more than treasury securities of comparable maturity. They can be purchased for a minimum amount of $25,000.

The stated maturity on a Ginnie Mae is usually 30 years, but an investor should expect it to have an average life of about ten years because most mortgages are paid off before maturity. Mortgagors can repay their debt, refinance, or default. In any case, investors receive a lump sum for the remaining portion of the principal.

Ginnie Maes are not risk-free. When interest rates fall, homeowners often refinance their mortgages. When refinancing occurs, investors receive their principal and interest payments sooner than expected. Holders of Ginnie Maes are then faced with reinvesting the payout at the prevailing lower rates.

The best way for small investors to participate in this market is to buy shares in a no-load mutual fund with minimum investments starting at $1,000. Remember that like bonds your yield is not fixed in a fund. Your yield will go up or down in accordance with changes in the general level of interest rates.

Before selecting a fund, always read the prospectus to determine the composition of its portfolio, sales fees and other charges, and previous return history. Most funds pay a monthly dividend from the interest on the securities but channel principal repayments back into the fund for more Ginnie Maes. Some good no-load fund choices include Benham GNMA Income Fund (800-321-8321), T. Rowe Price GNMA Fund (800-638-5660), or Vanguard GNMA (800-6627447).

Not all funds are equally affected by declining interest rates. Some funds seek to maximize current income by buying mortgage-backed securities with particularly high current yields. This strategy exposes the fund to high pre-payment risk when interest rates are falling. By contrast, other mortgage funds such as the Vanguard GNMA Fund tend to buy lower-coupon (interest rate expressed as an annual percentage of face value) mortgage securities, which reduces the prepayment risk while cutting into current income. In determining how exposed a mortgage fund is to prepayment risk, you can ask a fund for its average weighted coupon rate. The higher the rate, the greater the prepayment risk.

32

CONVERTIBLE SECURITIES

A convertible security is either a convertible bond or convertible preferred stock that can be exchanged into common stock at your discretion. Once it has been exchanged or converted into common stock, it cannot be converted back. If the security is a convertible bond, it provides you with a fixed interest payment. If the security is convertible preferred stock, it provides you with a stipulated dividend. What makes these securities attractive investments is that they can be redeemed for the company's common stock at a fixed price. This provision means the holders of these securities can reap the benefits of rising stock prices.

Convertible bonds generally have a face or par value of $1,000 when the bond matures. In addition, the corporation also pays a fixed rate of interest, which is usually less than the interest on a nonconvertible bond because of the value of the conversion feature. Investors are willing to receive a lower rate of interest in return for the opportunity to participate in the appreciation of the common stock.

Convertible preferred stock is not as common as convertible bonds. Most convertible preferred stock is issued as a result of mergers to provide income to holders of the security without diluting the common stock of the acquiring firm. Convertible preferred stock is similar to convertible bonds in that it is a hybrid combining a preferred stock issue and common stock. These stockholders' rights are subordinate to those of bondholders in a corporate liquidation; however, dividends must be paid on preferred stock before any dividends can be paid to common stockholders. Similar to convertible bonds, they provide a fixed dividend while still allowing participation in the appreciation of the price of the common stock through the right of conversion.

Advantages to the Investor. These securities combine the advantages of the safety and fixed income of bonds or preferred stock with the potential for capital appreciation from holding the common stock. The owners of these securities can participate in the rising price of the common stock by converting the security into that common stock. Actually, holders of these securities don't have to convert their securities to participate in rising stock prices. Typically, the price of the convertible security will rise with the price of the stock, although it never rises as much. On the other hand, if the stock price declines, the price of the convertible will also decline, again by not as much. In this case, the interest specified on the convertible bond or the dividend on the convertible preferred stock serves to brake the decline in price. Therefore, holders of convertible securities have good reasons to stay with the security and not convert.

Meanwhile, even if the stock price languishes, holders of these securities receive their guaranteed fixed return. Many of the companies issuing these securities are smaller companies whose common stock is speculative in nature. Many of these companies have a low dividend yield (cash dividend per share) on their common stock which makes the common stock an unattractive investment if current return is important to the investor. Convertible securities provide investors with an alternative way to participate in the possible appreciation of the stock while earning a good current return.

As a general rule, convertible securities are callable, which means a company can call in the security and redeem it for cash. Seldom are they actually redeemed. The purpose of the call provision is to force conversion of the issue when the conversion value of the security is significantly above the call price. If the convertible security is called when the market value of the stock is greater than the conversion value of the bond, conversion is advisable.

Outlook for Convertibles. Convertibles can be interesting investment vehicles. Their issuers are often small companies with excellent future prospects. In 1995, more than 600 companies had a total of nearly $90 billion in convertibles outstanding. A typical issuer is a young company with a market capitalization (price per share × number of shares outstanding) of about $450 million.

Convertibles continue to be a good source of steady income. The common stocks of convertibles only pay a dividend yield of 1.4 percent while the companies' convertibles pay an average yield of 6.5 percent.

As previously mentioned, most convertibles are issued by smaller companies and the performance of convertibles will tend to parallel the return of small-company stocks. If small-company stocks rally, a conservative alternative to buying these stocks is to purchase convertible stock funds.

Convertibles will do very well if there is a sustained rebound in small-stocks. However, if small-stock performance fizzles, convertible bond investors shouldn't get hit as hard as those who invest in small-stock funds. You can expect that convertibles will fall only about 40 percent as much as the drop in the underlying common stock while rising about 70 percent as high as that stock. For example, the Dow Jones Industrial Average rose 22.8 percent in the period from January 1, 1995 to July 30, 1995. Meanwhile, convertibles rose 15.62 percent over the same period.

In shopping for a convertible, the investor should focus on the prospects for the underlying common stock. Don't buy a convertible unless you believe the common stock is an attractive investment.

The safest way to invest in convertibles is to buy one of the 39 convertible mutual funds, up from only seven in 1982. Many large fund families have convertible funds. The $1 billion Fidelity Convertible Securities Fund (800-544-8888) has compiled an excellent record since its introduction in 1988.

33

DOLLAR-COST
AVERAGING

Peter Lynch, formerly portfolio manager of Fidelity Magellan, a top-performing mutual fund, says that predicting the short-term direction of the stock market is futile. In his book *One Up on Wall Street*, he writes that investors should concentrate on picking stocks and not attempt to predict the market as a whole. Over the long haul, it can be costly not to invest in common stocks. The approximately 10 percent average yearly return since 1926 indicates how profitable stock investments are in the long run. Over that period, common stocks have more than doubled the return that could have been on corporate bonds, government bonds or treasury bills and more than tripled the rate of inflation.

The longer the time period, the less risk there is of losing money investing in a diversified portfolio of common stocks. If an investor holds a basket of stocks that match the performance of Standard & Poor's 500-stock Index, the chance of losing money in any given year over the past 75 years was about 30 percent. However, over ten years, the risk of loss falls to just 3 to 4 percent. If you approach the market as an investor rather than as a trader, your chance of making long-term solid returns are excellent.

However, some important caveats should be stated. Before investing in common stocks, investors should have at least three to six months of living expenses in an account at the bank or a money-market fund. Individuals should also build up equity in a home to provide some protection against inflation as well as a nest egg that can be cashed in at retirement. Money needed in the near future for things such as college tuition payments or retirement funds should not be invested in the stock market. The stock market may plunge in value just when you need the funds. And don't forget to have adequate health and medical insurance.

Individuals leery of investing in common stocks can purchase no-load mutual funds that invest in common stock. Mutual funds provide the investors with the twin advantages of professional management and diversification.

Many investors are so concerned about the volatility of the stock market that they are afraid to buy common stocks or invest in mutual funds. In addition, reported abuses by insiders and traders have made many investors uneasy. How should the individual investor react? Very simply, every investor should focus on the long run. The American economy will continue to grow and corporations will continue to prosper. Ownership of common stock or mutual funds that invest in common stock gives investors a direct stake in the future of American corporations.

Given the difficulty of predicting market turns, what strategy should an investor follow in buying common stock or mutual funds? One of the oldest and best formula plans is what is called dollar-cost averaging. Dollar-cost averaging requires that an investor commit a fixed amount of funds to stocks or mutual funds at specific time intervals: monthly, quarterly, or whatever period is most convenient with the investor's saving schedule. The technique is very mechanical, requiring no forecast of the direction of the market. It is not a trading system, but a long-term investment program. Fixed amounts should be invested out of current income.

Under this program, the average cost of stocks or mutual funds in a portfolio should be less than the average market price. This occurs because a constant amount of dollars purchases fewer shares at higher prices and more shares at lower prices. A simple example illustrates this. Suppose you invest $1,200 every three months over the next year. Assume the price of the stock is $60 the first quarter, $40 the second, $60 the third, and $40 in the last quarter. The first quarter you would have bought 20 shares at $60 per share for a total of $1,200. The second quarter's investment of $1,200 would buy 30 shares. At the end of four quarters, you will have acquired 100 shares with your $4,800 investment, which means their average cost is $4,800 divided by 100 shares of $48. However, the average price of the stock during that year was $50.

Although this formula works best with stocks (or mutual funds) that fluctuate substantially, investors should avoid high-risk stocks. Buy quality stocks that will continue to produce above-average growth in revenues and earnings. Dollar-cost averaging is not a successful strategy when prices continue to move downward.

A free brochure titled *Dollar Cost Averaging* is available by contacting T. Rowe Price Associates (800-638-5660).The Vanguard Group (800-662-7447) also provides a free booklet titled *The Dollar-Cost Averaging Brochure.*

Dollar-cost averaging is easily implemented by participating in an automatic investment plan. For example, Vanguard sponsors a free service called Vanguard Fund Express. With Vanguard Fund Express, an amount you stipulate is electronically transferred from your bank account and invested in your Vanguard account on a regular basis. The amount can be as little as $50 up to $100,000, and it can be invested monthly, bimonthly, quarterly, semi-annually, or annually in the Vanguard Fund of your choice.

This plan greatly simplifies dollar-cost averaging. Your money is transferred directly and automatically on any day you select. Saving becomes easier because you never see the money. If you want to stop or change this automatic investment plan, all you have to do is send a letter detailing your new instructions.

34

COMPOUNDING

The English economist John Maynard Keynes referred to compound interest as "magic." Compound interest is interest on interest that compounds when it remains in the account, becoming part of the principal that earns further interest. The magic in compounding is the tremendous rate at which savings can mount over the years. The following table shows how $10,000 invested in a corporate bond providing 10 percent interest paid semi-annually can more than quadruple in value in only 15 years.

It is important to remember that compounding works for you only if interest or dividends are reinvested. If you buy a bond and do not reinvest the interest received, then the principal remains constant. In the previous example, if the interest is not reinvested, the interest each period is based on the $10,000 rather than on the $10,000 plus the accumulated interest. Interest on $10,000 for 15 years at 10 percent payable semiannually accumulates to only $15,000 if not reinvested. In other words, the $10,000 original investment would total $25,000 ($10,000 + $15,000) at the end of 15 years. The effect of compounding adds $18,2119 ($43,219 − $25,000) to the total.

Interest and dividends do not have to be reinvested in the same security. If better investment opportunities are available as interest or dividend payments are received, take advantage of them. The simplest way to reinvest your returns is to purchase shares of a mutual fund that provide automatic reinvestment of interest earned.

Dividend Reinvestment Plans. Dividend Reinvestment Plans (DRIPS) enable investors who already own shares of a company's stock to purchase additional shares by automatically reinvesting their dividends. Over a thousand companies, both large and small, have DRIPS. These companies typically charge at most a nominal fee that is substantially less than the commission you would have to pay to buy additional shares from a broker. In addition, you are often allowed to buy the shares at a discount from the current market price. For more information, read *Buying Stocks Without a Broker* by Charles B. Carlson, McGraw-Hill, 1992.

Rule of 72. A simple way to calculate how long it will take to double your investment if interest and dividends are reinvested is the Rule of 72. Simply divide 72 by the interest rate and you get the number of years it will take to double your money. For example, if the interest rate is 7 percent, dividing 72 by 7 percent means that it will take 10.3 years to double your money.

COMPOUND INTEREST ON A 10 PERCENT
$10,000 INVESTMENT

Time	Semiannual Interest	Cumulative Growth
6 months	$500	$10,500
1 year	525	11,025
1½ years	551	11,576
2 years	579	12,155
2½ years	608	12,763
3 years	638	13,401
3½ years	670	14,071
4 years	704	14,775
4½ years	739	15,514
5 years	776	16,290
5½ years	815	17,105
6 years	855	17,960
6½ years	898	18,858
7 years	943	19,801
7½ years	990	20,791
8 years	1,040	21,831
8½ years	1,092	22,923
9 years	1,146	24,069
9½ years	1,193	25,272
10 years	1,264	26,536
10½ years	1,324	27,860
11 years	1,393	29,253
11½ years	1,462	30,715
12 years	1,536	32,215
12½ years	1,613	33,864
13 years	1,693	35,557
13½ years	1,778	37,335
14 years	1,866	39,201
14½ years	1,960	41,161
15 years	2,058	43,219

35

LIFE INSURANCE

Shopping for life insurance can easily be one of life's more confusing tasks. Consumers are faced with a bewildering variety of new policies. Making the right choice involves careful study.

For many people, life insurance is an essential part of their financial planning. Nearly nine in ten families in the United States have some form of life insurance to meet the future needs of dependents, such as a spouse, a child, or an elderly parent. Increasingly, however, people are purchasing life insurance to build up cash reserves for a future event or expense, such as retirement or college tuition.

Although there are a bewildering variety of policies, the basic types can be identified as follows:

- Whole life insurance (often referred to as straight life or permanent life) is protection that can be kept in force as long as you live. Policyholders pay fixed monthly or annual premiums and heirs receive fixed death benefits. Meanwhile, policies earn interest, building cash values that can be withdrawn or borrowed.
- Term life is protection that insures your family for a specified period of time. A term insurance policy pays a benefit only if you die during the period covered by the policy. If you stop paying premiums, the insurance stops.

Term insurance is cheaper than whole life for the same amount of protection and gives you the largest immediate coverage per dollar. As a result, it is useful for those consumers who need large amounts of coverage for a known period of time. These groups include home buyers, parents of young children or people with high current debt.

- Universal life was the big innovation of the 1980s. You can increase or decrease premiums, depending on how large a cash value you want to build and how large you want the death benefit to be. The amount of cash value reflects the interest earned at the prevailing interest rates.
- Variable life insurance works like a mutual fund. You choose how to invest your premiums in a portfolio of stocks, bonds, or other assets. Thus, the death benefit and cash value will depend upon how well investments do.

Formerly, nearly all policies sold were whole life. They still account for nearly half the market. Insurance agents push them because they generate very high commissions for the agents. But what benefits the agent may not be best for you. Whole life builds cash value tax-free, but many policies pay niggardly interest rates. Most investors would be better off buying cheaper term coverage and investing the difference in no-load mutual funds.

How much insurance should you buy? This question is not easily answered. Financial advisers frequently disagree on how much is enough. When asked by *The Wall Street Journal* to evaluate the life insurance needs of a hypothetical 45-year-old corporate manager, ten advisers and insurance sellers gave answers that ranged from as little as $250,000 to as much as $1,250,000.

There is no simple answer to the question of how much insurance is enough because it is so dependent upon individual circumstances. An old rule of thumb is that life insurance coverage should equal five to seven times a person's annual salary. Unfortunately, the multiples only provide rough estimates, which may be totally inappropriate for a particular family's needs and goals. For example, single people generally don't need life insurance, but primary breadwinners in a family with children might need ten times their annual salary.

In 1990 the financial woes of First Executive Corp., the troubled California-based life insurance company, caused concern about the financial health of some of the nation's life insurance companies. What criteria should people use to judge an insurer's safety?

The first step is to look at the rating from A.M. Best Co. Although the company has been criticized for giving its highest rating (A+), too freely, use the Best rating as a first cut. There is little reason for buyers to consider insurance other than that of life insurers who hold the top Best rating.

The next step is to determine if an insurer is rated by Standard & Poor's Corp., Duff & Phelps Inc., and Moody's Investors Service Inc. These agencies are stingier about giving their maximum triple-A ratings than Best is in giving out its highest rating. The problem is that only a minority of insurers are rated by these agencies. Cautious buyers might want to use companies that get one of the three top grades from at least two of the evaluators. This criterion would rule out a company rated less than double-A-minus by S&P and Duff & Phelps and Aa-3 by Moody's.

Reports by Best, S&P, Moody's and Duff & Phelps are too expensive for most individuals to buy. However, this information can usually be obtained from your agent or your local public library. For further information, you can contact Weiss Research and have Weiss send you a financial evaluation of your insurance company (800-289-9222). The cost is $15.

Where can you get the best price for insurance? It is easy to compare the first-year premium of different policies. However, this information doesn't give you a true picture of the cost of insurance over your life. A more revealing figure is a number called the interest-adjusted net cost index. That index is an industry-accepted method for determining the true cost of insurance to the buyer in the long run. If factors in not only the premium, but also the interest, any dividends, and the timing of payments and receipts.

This complicated calculation should be provided by your insurance agent. In most states, companies are required to furnish that information if requested by the customer.

An unbiased evaluation of an insurance proposal can be obtained from the National Insurance Consumer Organization (NICO). For a fee, NICO will give you an opinion of your policy and even suggest a better choice. Call 202-574-6426 if you are interested.

Both Lifequote in Miami (800-521-7873) and Selectquote in San Francisco (800-343-1985) will send you no-obligation quotes on five of the cheapest term policies that meet your requirements. These services receive a commission from the insurer if you buy through them.

36

ANNUITIES

Annuities are confusing to many investors, but basically they amount to an unlimited, although nondeductible Individual Retirement Account (IRA). You purchase an annuity contract either with one large payment—a single premium policy or smaller monthly ones. Those that are similar to mutual funds are called "variable" annuities, because returns to the investors "vary" according to fund performance. Annuities that are more like certificates of deposit (CDs) are called "fixed" annuities because they pay a fixed rate of return for a specified period of time.

Annuity earnings accumulate tax free. Like an IRA, you pay tax on the interest only when you withdraw the money. After a set time, the insurer pays back your contributions plus the earnings that have accumulated. You can take that money in a lump sum or spread the payments over a number of years. You can also choose to get monthly payments for the rest of your life. The insurer has to keep up those payments, even if your contributions and earnings are exhausted. However, the payments cease when you die, even if you haven't collected as much as you contributed.

Why are annuities tax-deferred? Their favored status comes from the value of the insurance feature—and insurance products have always been tax favored. Should you die, your beneficiary gets either the fund's current value or your original investment, whichever is greater.

Remember that although annuities are sold by banks and brokers, they are always backed by insurance companies. As a result, unlike CDs, they are not protected by federal deposit insurance. While state guaranty plans may cover some losses, protection limits vary. Investors buying any annuity have to be concerned with the financial soundness of the insurance company that under-writes it.

Buy an annuity only from a company that has been rated A+ by the insurance rating service, A.M. Best. In addition, check to see if the company has been rated by Standard & Poor's, Duff & Phelps, or Moody's Investors Service. These services are stingier than A.M. Best in giving their highest rating. The company should receive one of the three top grades given by these services; otherwise select another company.

Tax-deferred annuities are not short-term savings vehicles. Unlike an IRA, there are no limits on the amount one can invest in any given year, and investors don't have to start making withdrawals at age 70½. However, any earnings taken out earlier than age 59½ are subject to regular income taxes and a 10 percent federal penalty. In addition, although annuities don't have up-front sales fees, they do charge you surrender fees for early withdrawal. These surrender charges are typically 7 percent in the first year, declining one percentage point a year to zero after about the eighth year.

Don't buy an annuity if you expect to need the money within ten years. The tax benefits are frequently exceeded by the fees. Annuity charges are stiff by any standards. On top of the approximately .75 percent in advisory and other fees, insurance companies add a fee of .85 percent to 1.25 percent of assets annually for death benefits and expenses.

As previously mentioned, variable annuities are tax-deferred investments, underwritten by insurance companies, that permit you to invest money in a handful of stock, bond, and money market funds. If you buy a variable annuity, consider buying through mutual-fund companies that sell annuities directly to investors rather than through brokers.

Two companies with lower fees are Scudder Stevens & Clark (800-225-2470) and the Vanguard Group (800-662-7447). Annual contract and management fees on a variable annuity stock-market portfolio total .95 percent for the Vanguard annuity, 1.45 percent for the Scudder annuity. In addition Vanguard and Scudder also have no surrender fee, and because their annuities are sold directly over the phone, there are no brokers' commissions to be paid.

The long-term interest rate is a critical factor when buying fixed-rate tax-deferred annuities. But don't just buy the annuity with the highest first-year rate. A company offering you a high first-year rate might drop it significantly the second year and keep it there. Check its interest-rate history with your agent or the company directly. Older customers should not be receiving any more than .75 percent less than newer customers.

Because of their stiff fees, most investors would be better off buying a good no-load mutual fund than buying an annuity. Annuities aren't for everyone and are definitely only appropriate as long-term investments. They make more sense for investors with more than $10,000 to invest tax-deferred every year. Those investors with lesser amounts to invest should look for lower-cost vehicles to get tax-deferral, such as 401(k) plans and IRAs. It is always a good idea to fund your 401(k) plan to the maximum before considering any other investment.

A listing of interest rates of more than 180 fixed annuities can be obtained by sending $10 for one issue of the *Comparative Annuity Reports Newsletter,* Post Office Box 1268, Fair Oaks, California 95628. The interest rates provided can be used as a basis of comparison with interest rates that are specified by an insurance agent. In addition, returns on variable annuities are computed by Lipper Analytical Source and are reported weekly in *Barron's.*

Morningstar (800-876-5005) will provide for $45 a single issue of *Morningstar Variable Annuity—Life Performance Report*, which gives a detailed evaluation of the relative performance of variable annuities.

Fidelity Investments has created a worksheet to help investors decide whether annuities are suitable investments for them. To request a copy, call 800-544-2442.

37

401(K) RETIREMENT PLANS

Named after the section of the federal law, the 401(k) plan is an outstanding way to build a retirement nest egg. Most large companies sponsor 401(k) plans or similar tax-deferred plans, and many smaller companies have recently adopted them. This plan provides employees with an automatic way to save for retirement while reducing and deferring taxes. Everyone should take advantage of this benefit whenever it is available.

A 401(k) plan is a retirement plan that permits you to defer paying taxes on a part of your salary. This contribution is deducted from your salary and is not counted as part of your earnings when it comes time to determine your income tax. The maximum tax-free deduction is adjusted each year for inflation. In 1995, the maximum deduction was $9,240. Taxpayers in the 28 percent bracket who made the maximum contribution of $9,240 saved $2,587 in federal taxes.

One of the most attractive features of 401(k) plans is that many companies match all or part of the employee contributions. They often, however, retain the option of claiming a portion of their matching contributions if the employee leaves the company within seven years.

A 401(k) is similar to an individual retirement account (IRA), but differs in some important respects. Both allow tax-deferred contributions to retirement. But with an IRA, you set up the account where you want and make your own investment choice. With a 401(k) plan, you are limited to the investment options the company provides. An IRA is limited to a maximum tax-deferred contribution of $2,000, and many workers don't qualify for any deduction on IRA contributions. In addition, there is no employer matching contribution with an IRA. However, if you can afford both, contribute to an IRA as well as a 401(k) plan.

As previously mentioned, the company chooses the investment options. The typical choices include the employer's stock, a stock mutual fund, a fund combining stocks and bonds, and so-called guaranteed investment contracts, or GICs, which are insurance contracts that pay a fixed rate of interest usually comparable to certificates of deposit.

Many people opt for the GIC option because they believe that these are the safest investments. That could be a big mistake. Locking in a guaranteed rate isn't worth giving up the potential price gains in common stock. Over a period of time, fixed-income returns may be seriously eroded by inflation. Shifting from fixed-income to stocks could easily double one's account in 20 to 30 years based upon the historical returns of common stock as compared to fixed-income returns.

Another mistake many employees make is to invest too much of their retirement-plan money in their own companies' stock. It is too risky to have your retirement nest egg too dependent upon a single stock.

Financial advisers generally recommend that people in their 20s and 30s invest a minimum of 70 percent of their retirement money in stock mutual funds. As you get older, you can gradually reduce the allocation. You also have the option of moving your money among the different investments at least once a year.

You can begin making 401(k) withdrawals without penalty after age 59½ or when you retire or are permanently disabled. You must begin withdrawing your 401(k) money by age 70½. The money can be withdrawn in a lump sum, but many plans also provide for the purchase of an annuity or installment payments. In any case, the withdrawals are subject to regular income tax.

You can withdraw funds before age 59½ only if you're facing a financial hardship or you need money for medical expenses that are greater than 7.5 percent of your adjusted gross income. To be eligible for early withdrawal, you may have to prove you have used up other financial resources before applying, and you can borrow only the amount you need.

Many plans do permit borrowing. Loans can be made for any reason the employer allows, and are not recognized as withdrawals because the money is scheduled to be paid back. Before borrowing against the plan, however, ask what the interest rate on loans is and how long before you have to repay the loan. Remember, moreover, that dipping into 401(k) funds to pay short-term expenses can put your retirement nest egg at risk.

One of the most basic investment mistakes many employees make is not joining 401(k) plans. About one-third of eligible employees are not participating. The younger employees are particularly apt to ignore these plans. They are making a big mistake. The 401(k) plan is positively the best investment vehicle for an employee. You get automatic savings, your contribution and its earnings are tax deferred, and you get free money from your employer. About 70 percent of all employers have set up some kind of matching program.

However small your contribution, everyone eligible should contribute to a 401(k) plan. Those employees who can afford to contribute the maximum should definitely do so. Take full advantage of this savings option before investing elsewhere.

38

IRAs

Here's a way to build a retirement nest egg that many investors fail to consider. More than 60 percent of all taxpayers still qualify for Individual Retirement Accounts (IRAs) that are fully or partly tax deductible. Those IRAs that remain deductible offer one of the best retirement plans available. Those that are not deductible at least enable you to build a retirement fund on a tax-deferred basis.

An IRA is a tax-advantaged account in which individuals invest money for their retirement. The return on the money invested is not subject to taxes until taken out at retirement. In other words, interest and dividend income is not taxed and accumulates on a tax-deferred basis until retirement.

Tax-deferred compounding of your earnings means that your IRA funds will grow more quickly and produce better end results than they would if the earnings were reduced every year by taxes. For example, if you invest $2,000 on January 1 every year and you are in the 28 percent bracket, the total amount accumulated at the end of 20 years would be $75,831 if fully taxed and $98,846 if earnings are tax-deferred.

Eligibility. You may invest in an IRA only if you or your spouse have earned income or receive alimony payments.

Individuals can contribute up to $2,000 a year out of earnings or alimony to an IRA. If both you and your spouse work, each of you can contribute up to the maximum of $2,000. A working and nonworking spouse can add an additional $250, meaning that their maximum contribution is $2,250.

If you or your spouse are not covered by an employer-sponsored retirement plan, you can tax-deduct the entire contribution. Even if you participate in an employer-sponsored pension plan, you get the full IRA tax deduction if your adjusted gross income does not exceed $40,000 if married or $25,000 if single. As your income increases, the amount you can deduct is reduced. The deduction finally phases out at $35,000 for singles and $50,000 for married couples.

IRAs may be opened with banks, credit unions, mutual funds companies, brokerage firms, or an insurance company. The wide variety of choices may include CDs, savings accounts, treasury securities, mutual funds, annuities, and individual stocks. Most people tend to go for low-risk investments. However, low risk usually means a low return, and that can easily be erased, over time, by inflation.

A common IRA mistake is to buy tax-exempt investments. Some examples are municipal bonds, municipal bond funds, and tax-exempt money-market funds. Because municipal securities are already tax-exempt, no additional savings can be realized from putting them in a tax-favored IRA. And since these securities pay a lower yield than taxable instruments, you reduce your potential return.

Withdrawals. Strict rules govern withdrawal of your funds from your IRA. You may withdraw funds from your IRA at any time without penalty once you have reached age 59½. You must begin to receive distributions from your IRA no later than April 1 following the year in which you turn age 70½.

In any case, you will have to pay income tax on the distributions.

If you withdraw money before age 59½, all the money taken out that was originally deductible will now be added to your income in the year it is taken out and taxed at your current tax rate. In addition, you will pay a 10 percent premature distribution penalty. It is to your advantage to defer withdrawals until age 70½. The longer you wait, the more your account will continue to grow tax-deferred.

If you're eligible for both an IRA and a 401(k) plan, invest first in the 401(k). It permits larger contributions, usually allows loans, and your employer will typically match your contribution. However, if you can afford it, by all means use both. Higher-income investors would probably be better off with municipal bonds than with IRAs because the interest received is permanently exempt from taxes.

39

REFINANCING A MORTGAGE

In the 1990s, the interest on 30-year fixed-rate mortgages was significantly below the rate that usually prevailed in the 1980s. Many financial advisers were suggesting that homeowners refinance. But refinancing is time consuming, and it also costs money. How can a decision be made?

The rule of thumb frequently used is that the difference between your mortgage interest rate and the current interest rate must be 2 percent or greater to justify refinancing your mortgage. However, this rule of thumb doesn't apply if you are going to own the house fewer than five years. When you add up all the costs and compare them with the prospective savings, it takes a minimum of about three years to even consider refinancing.

To avoid being financially penalized by a mistake made using this rule of thumb, some calculations need to be made. The biggest cost of refinancing is usually the bank's up-front fee, or what is called "points." Each point is equal to 1 percent of the mortgage. One-and-a-half to two points is a typical fee. On a $100,000 refinancing, you can expect to pay $1,500 to $2,000 for points.

Other costs need to be tallied. Lawyers' fees can run at least several hundred dollars. A new appraisal may be required along with miscellaneous fees for filing various documents. Many banks also charge an application fee of about $200.

Tax considerations are important. Under current tax law none of these refinancing costs is immediately deductible. Although points on an original mortgage are usually deductible in the tax year in which they are paid, points incurred refinancing must be amortized over the life of the loan.

The tax effects of the savings a borrower can expect from refinancing are also a factor. However, the after-tax savings may be less than you expect because a smaller mortgage payment usually means a smaller tax deduction for mortgage-interest payments.

One test to determine if it is worthwhile to refinance your mortgage used by Loantech (of Gaithersburg, Maryland) involves the following steps:

1. Current monthly principle and
   interest payment $_____
2. New monthly payment
   (available from lenders).   _____
3. Subtract line 2 from line 1   _____
4. How many months will you
   live here (maximum 120)   _____
5. Multiply line 3 by line 4   _____
6. Points and prepayment
   penalties paid   _____
7. Pre-tax difference
   (subtract line 6 from line 5)   _____
8. After-tax difference
   (multiply line 7 by .72 if you're
   in the 28 percent bracket,
   .67 if you're in the 33 percent
   bracket)   _____
9. Other closing costs   _____
10. Result of refinancing
    (subtract line 9 from line 8)   _____

A positive number in line 10 means refinancing will save you money.

You should call at least six lenders when shopping for a loan and ask them for the new rate, the monthly principal and interest payments, points, and prepayment penalties. Mortgage rates offered by local lenders are usually listed in the real estate section of the Sunday edition of your local newspaper.

40

FINANCIAL PLANNERS

A boom has been underway in the sale of financial advice in the 1990s. The number of firms registered as investment advisers with the SEC has increased from 17,400 in 1990 to 21,600 in 1994, with most of the growth coming from mom-and-pop operations that might employ just one or two people. Up to half of those registered have entered the business in the last decade.

The number of people taking the Certified Financial Planner exam, an industry credential, has zoomed from about 400 in 1992 to more than 2,000 in 1995. More than 30,000 people currently have C.F.P. designations, up by about 50 percent since 1990.

Charles Schwab Corporation has become a major factor in the boom of this industry. Schwab has $39 billion in assets managed by its financial advisers, up from $10 billion in 1992 and just $500 million in 1987. Schwab is eagerly trying to expand the market for its financial advisers. It hopes to make this an industry dominated by brand-name firms. To that end, it devised a program that it tested for two years in Florida and California. The program should be going nationwide in 1996 and it is intended to serve customers with $100,000 to invest.

Merrill Lynch, the nation's largest brokerage firm, is jumping on the same bandwagon. Its 11,700 brokers are now called "financial consultants," and Merrill Lynch is spending a great deal of money to enable them to live up to that designation.

In the past, many financial planners were getting paid by commissions. Unfortunately, this system often led to abuses such as recommending investments, like limited partnerships, that paid them more but also carried greater risks. Increasingly, planners are getting paid by charging fees that are not tied to specific investments. In 1987, for example, 64 percent of Certified Financial Planners were paid entirely by commissions; in 1994, only 19 percent were so paid. Free-only advisers are the fastest growing group in the industry. Many consumer advocates believe that paying fees rather than commissions reduces the potential for conflict of interest in promoting a particular investment.

Financial planning can be expensive—often several thousand dollars in hourly fees, commissions, or both—so shopping around is essential. Lower-cost alternatives might be available, including financial planning provided by an employer. Before committing to a planner, always get a written estimate of the cost of the planner's services. Unless your situation is complicated, you shouldn't have to pay more than 1 percent of the assets involved for a financial plan.

Finding a Planner. As a first step, make sure you understand the key credentials for financial advisers, including memberships in trade and professional groups. The key designations are as follows:

1. *C.F.P.* (*Certified Financial Planner*)—planners who have met educational and experience requirements, agree to abide by a code of ethics, and passed a written exam.
2. *R.I.A.* (*Registered Investment Adviser*)—anyone who has paid $150 to register with the SEC; required of most people who give advice about securities.
3. *A.I.C.P.A.-P.F.P.* (American Institute of Certified Public Accountant's-Personal Financial Planning Specialist)—certified public accountants who have passed a financial planning test, have practical experience in financial planning, and are members of the A.I.C.P.A.
4. *N.A.P.F.A.* (*National Association of Personal Financial Advisers*)—trade group representing fee-only financial advisers.

5. *I.A.F.P.* (*International Association for Financial Planning*)—broad-based trade group that seeks to serve all financial planners.

Generally, you should limit your search to those who have demonstrated their expertise by obtaining one of the designations. Although meeting the requirements does not guarantee competence, it does represent a good starting point in your search for the right planner.

The International Association for Financial Planning can assist you in finding a planner. If you call 800-945-4237, the association will send you at no cost:

- a list of up to five financial advisers in your area;
- a *Consumer Guide to Comprehensive Financial Planning*, which contains basic planning information and tips on choosing a planner;
- a financial adviser disclosure form that can be used when interviewing planners to evaluate their qualification and experience.

Another source of information on choosing a financial adviser is a booklet available free from Oppenheimer Funds by calling 800-456-1699.

41

YOUR ASSET ALLOCATION PLAN

A widely publicized 1994 study by Merrill Lynch showed that, with life expectancies increasing in the United States, many people are not saving enough to completely provide for their retirement. At the same time, outside support is diminishing. It is estimated that, by the year 2000, Social Security benefits will provide less than 20 percent of the retirement income for most people.

The study reported that the 76 million people born between 1948 and 1964 are saving only 38 percent of what they need to retire at age 65 without changing their lifestyles. Further, the average 50 year old has only about $2,300 in savings, and people in this country now save only about 4 to 5 percent of what they earn. Many other countries have savings rates two to three times our savings rate.

How should you prepare financially for your retirement? A key aspect is devising an appropriate investment program.

Short-Term Goals. Before you structure an investment program, you need to consider a short-term savings plan. This plan involves savings you may need within five years. You should have an emergency fund that covers three to six months' worth of living expenses. Self-employed or retired people might need up to a year's worth.

Where do you invest these short-term savings? These savings have to be accessible and safe. Money market funds, CDs, and Treasury bills are good choices.

Long-Term Investment Program. The critical step here is to develop an asset allocation program. Your asset allocation is the balance you assign to the three basic investment classes:

1. *Cash.* Cash includes money market funds and CDs as well as your savings and checking accounts. These choices provide a stable principal value and current interest income.
2. *Bonds.* Bonds are debt securities issued by corporations, the federal government and its agencies, and state and local governments. These securities offer higher interest income than cash reserves but their value fluctuates with changes in interest rates.
3. *Common Stocks.* Common stocks represent an ownership interest in a corporation. They often pay dividends and offer the potential for capital gains, but stock market risk is also present.

As previously mentioned, studies have shown that investment returns depend primarily upon how you divide your assets among the three investment classes. The specific stock, bond, or cash and cash equivalent choices you make are far less important.

Historically, common stocks have offered the highest return of the three investment classes. These returns reflect dividend income as well as capital gains. For example, in the period from 1926–1994, large company stocks (as measured by the Standard & Poor's 500 Index) returned 10.2 percent. Meanwhile, long-term government bonds returned 5.1 percent over the same period and U.S. Treasury bills (a good proxy for cash reserves) returned 3.7 percent.

To further illustrate the difference, if you had invested $10,000 in 1964 in each of the three classes, cash would have grown to $69,240, bonds to $75,200, and common stock to $171,940 (more than twice bonds or cash). Clearly, the higher your allocation to common stocks, the higher your return. But common stocks entail greater risk. In this century, the stock market has dropped more than 10 percent 53 times (about once every two years). It has dropped over 25 percent 15 times (about once every six years). These declines can be very unsettling to an investor. However, it is important to realize that time has a moderating influence on the risk of investing in common stocks. If your investment horizon is 20 years, the risk of investing your money in a diversified portfolio of common stocks (about 15 stocks) has historically been very low. If your time horizon is less than five years, a conservative investor might be better off avoiding common stocks altogether.

Smart investors avoid "market timing" strategies. Few investors can accurately foresee the direction of the stock or bond markets. The problem with market timing is that market rallies occur in brief spurts. Market timers are often out of the market when these brief spurts occur.

If you had invested $1,000 in Standard & Poor's 500 Index on January 1 of every year since 1965, your annual return would have been 11 percent. If you were unlucky enough to invest that $1,000 at the peak of the market each year, your annual return would have been 10.6 percent. The key to being a successful investor during this period was not market timing but staying invested in common stocks.

International Stocks. International stocks are an appropriate investment for even conservative investors. The market values of U.S. stocks make up about one-third of world equity values, and this ratio probably will continue to decrease in the future. Stock markets outside North America have done better, as a group, than the U.S. market in 16 of the past 25 calendar years (1970–1994). During this period, the Morgan Stanley Capital International Index, which reflects all major stock markets outside North America, gained 938 percent, with dividends in cash, while the U.S. index rose 331 percent. With dividends invested, international stock gained 2,126 percent while the U.S. index rose 1,082 percent.

Anywhere from 10 to 25 percent of your portfolio could be invested in international stocks. Allocating your assets over more markets should raise potential rewards while lowering your portfolio's risk. By investing abroad, you can participate in the markets of countries enjoying faster economic growth than the United States.

The best way to invest internationally is through the purchase of no-load mutual funds. Today most fund families have at least one international fund.

Model Portfolios. The model portfolios described are for the conservative investor and represent suggestions for different portfolio mixes based upon your age group. If your time horizon exceeds 20 years, a significant portion of your portfolio should be devoted to common stock (or stock funds). If your time horizon is between 10 and 20 years, you might begin lowering your risk by moving some of your assets into more conservative stocks and bonds (or bond funds). Even in retirement, however, your time horizon is long enough for stocks to have a place in your portfolio.

The portfolios are arranged according to four age groups:

25–40. Since you have a long time horizon, you can invest more of your money in common stocks with 80 percent of your portfolio in stocks or stock funds. To add diversification, some assets should be kept in low-risk cash equivalents (such as money market funds, CDs, or short-term bond funds).

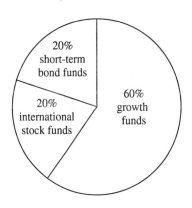

40–55. You still have a long-term time horizon but you might turn a bit more cautious. Lower your portfolio risk by increasing your allocation to money market mutual funds.

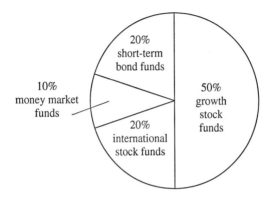

55–65. Although you are nearing retirement, your investment strategy should still focus upon growth of your assets. This model is 60 percent invested in stocks with the remainder in bonds and cash equivalents. You might include stocks where dividend income is a focus or buy a growth and income stock fund.

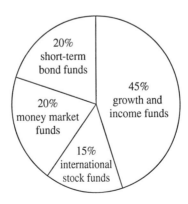

Over 65. You are now retired. Your two primary investment goals should be current income and the preservation of your capital but you should have some growth investments to keep up with inflation.

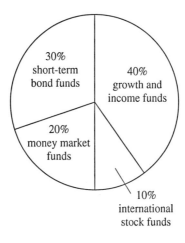

30%
short-term
bond funds

40%
growth and
income funds

20%
money market
funds

10%
international
stock funds

42

GOLD

From 1934 to 1971, the United States maintained a policy of buying and selling gold at a fixed price of $35 per ounce. Thus the U.S. dollar was regarded as a substitute for gold and, therefore, as "good as gold." For 37 years this policy prevailed until the Nixon administration suspended the dollar's convertibility into gold in 1971. There is no longer a link between gold and the international value of the dollar. The value of gold is now determined by market forces. In the 1970s the price of gold zoomed upward and peaked in 1980 at $570 an ounce before falling to $308 in 1984. Since 1984 its price has fluctuated in the neighborhood of $400.

Traditionally it has been said that an ounce of gold will buy a tailor-made man's suit. Surprisingly, this relationship has held for hundreds of years. Gold has been a remarkably constant source of value through time. For 5,000 years gold has been more of an alternative currency than a commodity and has been used as money. Its universal acceptability has been due to its relative scarcity as well as its glitter. In recent years, the output of gold has been spurred by modern production methods that can sift 50 tons of low-ore rock for the gold equivalent of a single one-ounce coin.

According to Gold Fields Mineral Service Ltd. of London, production in 1980 was 1,131 metric tons, while in 1994, it more than doubled to 2,250 metric tons. Interestingly, however, the demand for gold for use in jewelry over the same period went from 542 metric tons to more than 2,700 metric tons, a five-fold increase.

Jewelry sales now account for 75 percent of the world's gold output. The United States is still the world's largest customer, but China is running a close second. The Asian demand for gold will undoubtedly be a primary determinant of gold prices in the future.

Gold has usually been a barometer for confidence in political and currency stability. When inflation heats up, demand for gold increases, pushing its price upward. On the other hand, when prices are relatively stable, gold becomes less attractive. Purchases of gold surge when political events take a negative turn but a politically stable environment reduces the interest in gold. Finally, high interest rates on money market instruments and securities make them more attractive as investments than gold since gold ownership (in physical form) yields no interest. All of these factors make forecasting gold prices very difficult.

How to Purchase Gold. If an investor wants to buy gold to insure against economic instability or to diversify holdings, there are several avenues to pursue:

1. gold stocks
2. gold coins
3. gold mutual funds
4. gold bullion

Several different Canadian and American gold mining companies are traded on the New York Stock Exchange, American Stock Exchange, and the over-the-counter market. The price of these stocks rises or falls with changes in the price of gold. Since these stocks are traded on the exchanges, they can be readily bought and sold.

Gold coins are issued by several governments that guarantee their gold content. All gold coins are not the same. They come in various weights and sizes. Some have a pure gold content, and others consist of gold mixed with copper. Gold coins are sold at a price that reflects their gold value plus commission of from 5 to 8 percent. Prominent gold coins include the American Gold Eagle, Australian Nugget, Canadian Maple Leaf, Austrian 100 Corona, and the Gold Mexican 50 Peso.

Gold mutual funds provide several advantages to investors who want to invest in gold stocks but don't feel comfortable selecting individual stocks. These mutual funds handle the details of stock transactions. In addition, the managers have more time and experience to select from among gold stocks than most individual investors can afford. Finally, they provide the stability of investing in a portfolio of gold stocks versus the risk of investing in one or two gold stocks. Currently, there are 38 gold funds, seven of which are no-loads.

Some investors may choose to invest in gold bullion, which comes in many sizes ranging from a tiny wafer to 400 ounces. Most investors don't actually take physical possession of the bullion. Instead they purchase a certificate of ownership that indicates the gold is on deposit in a bank. Certificates can be purchased from certain banks, large brokerage houses, and recognized dealers. They are sold at about 3 percent over the price of the metal, and an annual storage fee is charged of approximately 1 percent. Benham Certified Metals has a discount brokerage division. The minimum purchase of gold is $2,000 (800-447-4653).

Is Gold a Smart Investment? Many experts recommend investing 5 to 10 percent of personal savings in gold. This advice seems reasonable when an investor wishes to diversify holdings or hedge against inflation or economic instability. However, investing a large percentage of assets in gold is not recommended. In the period from 1985 to 1994, the average gold mutual fund with a ten-year history gave a return of 96.90 percent while the stock market, as measured by the S&P 500 Index, tripled.

43

INVESTMENT CLUBS

One way for small investors to familiarize themselves with the investment markets at little cost is to join investment clubs. Investment clubs are groups of people—usually ten to 20—who get together to learn investment principles, build an investment portfolio, and exchange information with other members. The members of most groups meet once a month, deposit their monthly investments, typically $20 to $50, review studies of stocks presented by members, and select a stock in which to invest. The liquidation value of shares is computed regularly. A member may withdraw from the club and receive the liquidation value of his or her shares.

National Association of Investment Clubs (NAIC). Many of the clubs belong to the National Association of Investment Clubs, a nonprofit organization whose annual dues are $39 per club plus $14 for each member of the club. For this price you receive a manual that provides complete instructions for organizing and operating your investment club and assistance in the evaluation of stocks. In addition, you receive a monthly magazine, *Better Investing*—an excellent investment education publication.

The NAIC has three classes of membership: individual, investment club, and corporate. Currently, there are 54,000 individual members, 16,100 investment clubs with about 248,000 members, and about 235 corporate members. The average club is 9¼ years old with a portfolio of $90,000.

The NAIC lists four principles that provide a foundation for sound investing practice:

1. Invest a set sum once a month in common stock, regardless of general market conditions.
2. Reinvest dividends and capital gains immediately. Money grows faster if earnings are reinvested.

3. Buy growth stocks companies with sales and earnings increasing at an above-average rate.
4. Invest in different fields. Diversification helps spread both risk and opportunity.

Information about the NAIC can be obtained from:
    1515 East Eleven Mile Road
    Royal Oak, Michigan 48067
    810-583-6242

American Association of Individual Investors (AAII). Although, strictly speaking, it is not an investment club, the American Association of Individual Investors is an "independent, nonprofit corporation formed for the purpose of assisting individuals in becoming effective managers of their own assets through programs of education, information, and research." This estimable organization, composed of over 180,000 members, is an invaluable source of information to all investors regardless of their expertise. The $49 annual membership fee includes a subscription to the monthly *AAII Journal* and the annual *The Individual Investor's Guide to Low-Load Mutual Funds.*

The monthly magazine provides articles that should appeal to even the most sophisticated investor. They are written by prominent practitioners and academicians in different areas and reflect the latest thinking in the field. The annual guide to no-load funds is a comprehensive, easy-to-read comparison of more than 800 mutual funds. The data provided include a wide variety of risk and performance statistics of interest to investors.

In addition, the AAII has an investment home study program designed for those who want to enhance their understanding of investing. In ten lessons, it explores the concepts, strategies, and analytical methods that are useful for successful investing and portfolio management. The program costs $55 for members, and updates and revisions are sent free to members as they are developed.

Information about the AAII can be obtained from:
    P.O. Box 11092
    Chicago, Illinois 60611-9737
    312-280-0170

44

SOURCES OF INFORMATION

The purpose of this Key is to describe the primary sources of information available to assist investors in making decisions. An investor does not need to read all the sources to make informed choices. However, it is necessary to be aware of trends in the economy and business activity. Most successful investors have a broad knowledge of the business and investment environment, so they are capable of making judgments independent of the so-called experts. Such knowledge is important because the opinions of experts are frequently contradictory.

The most accessible source of information for nearly all investors is the financial pages of newspapers. Newspapers vary in their coverage of financial developments from excellent to poor. Both *The New York Times* and *USA Today* have excellent financial sections. Many investors choose to supplement their local newspapers with a specialized financial newspaper such as *The Wall Street Journal,* by far the most widely read daily financial newspaper. *Investor's Business Daily* is also useful, particularly to those investors who use technical analysis (predicting future stock prices by using charts).

There are also many general business periodicals and financial magazines available. *Business Week, Fortune,* and *Forbes* are three major business magazines. *Business Week* is oriented more towards news reporting than the other two periodicals. *Forbes* and *Fortune* (both published biweekly) focus on specific companies and business personalities. Investors should examine these periodicals and subscribe to at least one that appears useful in enhancing their understanding of the securities markets. *Barron's,* the weekly sister publication of *The Wall Street Journal,* provides a wealth of useful financial data as well as columns and features on events significant to investors. *Money* carries many articles on investments and is a useful source of information on all aspects of financial planning.

Forbes, Business Week, and *Money* regularly devote issues to mutual funds. In the fall of each year, *Forbes* has an honor roll for mutual funds that have been the most successful performers. *Kiplinger's Personal Finance Magazine* gives excellent coverage to mutual fund investing. Every quarter, *Barron's* prints Lipper Analytical Services' mutual fund performance data plus numerous articles on mutual fund investing. Both Morningstar and Value Line publish publications that track thousands of mutual funds. These services are expensive; however, they are available at many public libraries.

Standard & Poor's and Moody's are the two most important firms in the investment information business. They compete with a broad array of products covering the entire investment arena. Standard & Poor's publishes a series of *Standard Stock Reports,* which is usually available at brokerage firms. These one-page reports provide a useful summary and description of a firm's operations and financial history. For investors in bonds, it publishes the *Bond Guide,* which provides relevant information on thousands of corporate and convertible bonds.

Probably the most influential single stock advisory service is *The Value Line Investment Survey.* This publication is often available at public libraries. It provides a one-page summary of useful financial data on individual companies. Included is a ranking of timeliness and safety on a one to five scale. Timeliness is the probable price performance relative to the market over the next twelve months. Safety is the stock's future price stability and the company's current financial strength. A rank of 1 is the highest. This systematic approach lets the investor know exactly how *Value Line* regards the prospects of each firm.

Two monthly publications of note are *Worth* and *SmartMoney.* Both of these magazines provide excellent advice about investment strategy and recommendations of stocks, bonds, and mutual funds.

45

INVESTMENT SCAMS

Every year the financial media report on some investment scam that has duped unwary investors. The annual take through lying and deceit is in the billions of dollars. Successful investment swindlers use every trick in the book to steal your hard-earned dollars. Typically, they offer you a once-in-a-lifetime opportunity to make a lot of money quickly. To protect yourself, check out any person or firm with whom you intend to invest; examine every investment offer carefully; and continue to monitor any investment you make. You should be suspicious of any get-rich-quick scheme. If an opportunity is so unique, why would someone want to share the anticipated riches with you?

Ponzi Schemes. A 30-year-old immigrant, Charles Ponzi, etched his name in the annals of history in 1920 when he made an offer thousands of investors could not refuse: a 50 percent return in just six weeks. By the time the scheme began to unravel six months later, Ponzi had pocketed $10 million. His name has become synonymous with confidence games in which some early investors earn excellent returns, paid off with funds obtained from later participants in a scheme, who lose everything.

Variations on the Ponzi scheme have duped investors over and over again. When the demand for new participants exhausts the supply, the Ponzi pyramid collapses, crushing the hopes of its "investors."

Other Scams. Another variation of the Ponzi scheme is the illegal pyramid scheme involving Multilevel Marketing companies. MLMs have as their primary goal the signing up of thousands of salespeople who pay for the privilege of signing up even more salespeople hoping to share in their commissions. Many MLMs become illegal pyramid schemes when distributors primarily generate their revenues by collecting fees for signing up new distributors, who in turn collect fees by bringing in still more distributors. Selling the product is actually a secondary purpose of some MLMs.

Investment talk-radio shows have become an important source of scams. Thousands of investors have lost millions of dollars while buying investments in second mortgages, stamps, coins, and wireless cable. In Los Angeles, 1,500 investors lost $30 million after hearing second mortgages fraudulently touted on a local radio show. Among the victims were engineers, business owners, and corporate middle managers.

Advertisements appear on many investment shows for get-rich-quick schemes for wireless cable, coins, and commodities. Some radio stations are pressuring legitimate broadcasters to broadcast commercials advertising these schemes.

Before buying an investment discussed on the radio, find out if you have tuned into a long infommercial, paid for by a promoter. If you are suspicious, call the station.

Any investment that promises you extraordinary returns should be regarded with extreme caution. Fraud seems to be rampant in such areas as art, coins, gold, and limited partnerships. The penny stock (stocks selling for less than one dollar a share) market has been a continuing source of headaches to state securities regulators. An estimated $2 billion a year is lost by speculators in penny stocks. Penny stocks should be avoided entirely by conservative investors.

The emergence of computerized dialing and cheap long-distance phone rates has allowed smooth-talking brokers working out of "boiler rooms" to contact millions of people. Never send money to a stranger who calls you on the phone offering a "hot tip."

Although many scams are associated with the promise of extraordinary returns, others promise safety—an investment that can't miss! In one highly publicized case, the SEC found that hundreds of investors were bilked out of millions of dollars through buying phony municipal bonds sold by FSG Financial Services Inc. in Beverly

Hills. The firm was closed in July 1991, after the SEC filed a civil suit in federal court in Los Angeles accusing the firm of the fraudulent sale of securities.

If you have doubts about a securities firm, or if you want information about violations by brokers, check with the National Association of Securities Dealers, who can be reached at 800-289-9999, and the Securities Investor Protection Corporation, at 202-371-8300.

If you are concerned about a particular company or individual, contact the attorney general of your state and your local state's attorney to see if they have received complaints. They are useful sources of information about investment swindles and other scams.

The best strategy is to be vigilant when you are promised a substantially higher rate of return than the prevailing return. Never allow yourself to be sucked into an investment based upon an urgent plea for quick action before it is too late. You would never make a purchase of a car after a ten-minute consideration. Almost everyone who is in the market for a new automobile does some reading, talks to others, visits various showrooms, and the like. Any investment deserves the same careful consideration.

Don't be impressed by a smooth delivery. If the pitch sounds suspicious, you would do well to forget it. Stick to the basic types of investment vehicles described in this book.

46

INVESTMENT TIPS

Investing profitably is a lot easier than most investors realize. Successful investing is not determined by your picking the right individual stocks or correctly calling market turns. These tasks are complicated and even the so-called experts have little success predicting market turns.

To be a successful investor, you must have clear objectives and guidelines. If you are investing for growth, substantial investment in public utility stock doesn't make much sense. You should be looking for stocks with earnings that are expected to increase rapidly or mutual funds specializing in such stocks. Income investors should buy bonds or stocks that have a high dividend yield or mutual funds that seek investments producing high current income.

Certain strategies have been very successful in the past. By following these strategies, investors can avoid some of the most common errors. The following rules should guide you in your investment planning;

1. *Don't time the stock market.* Every study has shown that the chances of anticipating stock market moves up or down are very slim. Historically, the stock market has gone up two out of every three years. Although bear markets can see steep declines in stock prices, they tend to be of significantly shorter durations than bull markets. Bull markets tend to be of longer durations than bear markets. However, bull market gains are usually compressed into a very short time period. You don't want to be out of the market when these surges occur.

2. *Long-term investors (even conservative ones) should structure a portfolio dominated by stocks or stock mutual funds.* Over the last 70 years, stocks have

rewarded investors with an average compounded annual return of 10 percent, about 7 percent better than the rate of inflation. In contrast, government bonds have beat inflation by about 1.3 percent, and treasury bills barely beat inflation by about .4 percent. If you want the real value (adjusted for inflation and taxes) of your investment portfolio to increase, stocks are the place to be. As an aggressive investor, you might allocate 65 percent of your higher portfolio to stocks, 20 percent to bonds and 15 percent to cash (bank or money market accounts). A more conservative approach is to allocate 40 percent of your portfolio to stocks, 30 percent to bonds, and 30 percent to cash. Whatever you prefer, stock or no-load mutual funds that invest in stock should be an important part of your portfolio.

3. *Buy no-load mutual funds.* Suppose you put $1,000 into a 5 percent load stock fund. Because of the 5 percent load, only $950 gets invested in your name. The $50 represents a sales charge; none goes to the managers of the fund. In other words, it doesn't serve to improve the performance of the managers by providing them with an extra incentive.

All studies show that load funds do not outperform no-load funds. Future performance is uncertain, but the immediate savings from avoiding a sales charge is a known quantity. Why put yourself at a disadvantage by paying a sales charge?

This reasoning applies to all the other charges that some mutual funds impose such as redemption fees and 12b-1 fees. All these fees reduce your returns. Why pay them when there are many mutual funds that don't charge them?

No-load stock mutual funds should be the key to the investment strategy of most investors. For advice on which funds to buy, read *Forbes, Money, Business Week, Kiplinger's Personal Finance Magazine, Fortune, SmartMoney*, or *Worth.* All of these magazines provide information on the past performance of mutual funds and recommendations on mutual funds to buy now.

4. *Diversify.* Well-diversified portfolios—including various mixes of stocks, bonds, cash equivalents like treasury bills or money funds, and sometimes other types of investments can reduce a lot of the ups and downs in investing. And studies reveal that over lengthy periods, investors don't have to sacrifice much in the way of returns to get that reduced volatility.

If you were interested in making as much money as possible, and your time horizon was 30 years, then you could justify putting all your money in stocks. But most investors have shorter-term horizons, and the stock market can go down over the short run. For them, having their assets in a mixture of stocks, bonds, cash equivalents, and real estate (at least their own home) is a better approach. Even a simple strategy, such as allocating 60 percent to stocks, 35 percent to bonds, and 5 percent to cash, would have produced an average annual return of about 10 percent since 1965.

For most investors, no-load mutual funds are the best way to diversify their savings. Those investors who like to select their own stocks should remember that it takes a minimum of about 15 different stocks to make a well-diversified portfolio. Make sure the stocks chosen are from a variety of industries. The basic objective is to always have some stocks that do well to offset others that are lagging.

5. *Dollar cost average.* Trying to time stock market moves is almost always futile. A large portion of the gains in a bull market often occur in a short time span. These gains often come when there is great uncertainty about the future course of the stock market and the economy. All too often, stock market timers are on the sidelines while the market surges ahead. What should a skittish investor do? One answer is to allocate dollar amounts to a stock (or mutual fund) at regular intervals, usually monthly or quarterly.

By sticking to an automatic investment schedule, you avoid the greatest hindrance to investment success: your emotions. Your emotions will typically lead you to buying shares when prices are rising and to stop buying or even sell when they fall.

With dollar-cost averaging, investors automatically buy more shares when prices are lower and fewer shares when prices are high. As a result, the average cost of the shares you buy is usually lower than the average price during the period.

This technique works best for long-term investors. Long-term investors can ignore the occasional war, interest-rate spike or industry meltdown. You must have faith that over the long term, the U.S. economy will thrive and stock prices will rise, just as they have done in the past.

5. *Reinvest dividends and interest.* The basic objective in investing in securities is to earn an attractive, fully compounded rate of return. This requires regular reinvestment of interest, dividends, and capital gains. Compounding interest and dividends is the safest, most certain way to increase your wealth. If you had invested $1,000 in the S&P index at the beginning of 1926, for example, the investment would be worth over $50,000 today if you withdrew the dividends every year. If the dividends were reinvested in new shares, your $1,000 investment would have grown to more than $800,000.

When you invest in a mutual fund, you can elect automatic reinvestment of dividends and capital gains in your mutual fund. When the fund pays dividends or distributes capital gains, the mutual fund manager immediately invests this money in more securities. There's no cost, it is convenient, and your money compounds much more rapidly.

More than 1,000 major corporations offer shareholders the option of taking their dividends in the form of more shares of the company's stock. If you own stock in a company offering a dividend reinvestment plan (DRIP), take advantage of it.

47

INITIAL PUBLIC OFFERINGS (IPOs)

Netscape is a maker of software that enhances the ability to conduct business on the Internet. On August 9, 1995 Netscape "went public" (the phrase that is used when a private company first offers its shares to the public) in an initial public offering (IPO) at a price of $28 per share. It promptly zoomed from 28 to 75 and closed that day at 58½.

Although Netscape is an extreme example, many other IPOs have sold at large premiums over the offering price. In the period from January 1 to October 1 in 1995, new issues soared, gaining an average 23 percent in their first four weeks of trading. Although these gains are certainly enticing, conservative investors should be wary of participating in this risky market.

Although some new issues continue to surge after day one, big first-day jumps followed by mediocre performances have historically been the pattern. Two college professors, Tim Loughran and Jay Ritter, studied the performance of 4,753 IPOs from 1970 to 1990. If the first-day gains of those stocks are deducted from their returns, their average performance was significantly less than that of other companies of similar size. From the first through the fifth year after issue, the average annual returns of the IPOs trailed the stocks of other companies of similar size by a steep seven percentage points.

Small investors often are not able to buy an IPO at the initial offering price so they jump in after it is trading and pay a stiff premium. Eventually the stock price settles down and the small investor is stuck with a stock providing mediocre returns.

Wall Street syndicate managers estimate that institutions purchase about 60 percent of the typical IPO deal and 80 percent of the hot deals. In a normal deal, individuals might be allocated 25 percent of the shares, whereas in an exciting offering they might only receive five percent of the shares. After the institutions rake in their shares, there's little left to divvy up among individuals. Unfortunately, the way the system works is that the easiest offerings for individuals to participate in are those the institutions don't want to touch. These offerings are often of dubious quality.

Why do IPOs underperform after a short time? Several possible answers exist. One reason has to do with SEC regulatory requirements. Company insiders with restricted stock are prohibited from selling their shares until 180 days has elapsed from the offering date. Once the prohibition period has expired, insiders start selling and prices weaken.

Another reason is that underwriters time the sale to coincide with peaks in the market and industry cycles. Thereafter, the company's stock doesn't seem as attractive.

These factors suggest a strategy to reduce the risk of entering this market. Wait a year after issuance before considering the purchase of an IPO. A year should be long enough to lessen the risk of investing in a bad new issue, while getting you in early enough to participate in the gains a successful company can generate in the long run.

QUESTIONS AND ANSWERS

Should I use a discount broker?

If you don't seek or want advice, you should consider using discount brokers. The biggest advantage is the lower commission costs. Customers of discount brokers can expect to pay about half the commission charged by a full-service broker. Discount brokers are able to offer these lower rates because they do not provide research. Salaried order clerks handle the transactions rather than commissioned brokers, and they maintain low overhead. Discount brokers work on salary rather than on commission. Their purpose is to execute transactions, not persuade you to invest by making a sales pitch. Their income is not dependent upon the number of trades investors make. Like full-service brokers, discount firms will send investors confirmations of orders and monthly statements and will safeguard their certificates if desired.

What are redemption fees and 12b-1 plans?

Until recently, mutual funds were either load or no-load. But today fee structures are more complex and confusing to investors. Among these fees are redemption fees, also called contingent deferred sales charges or back-end loads. This fee is charged when investors sell their shares, usually within a fixed period. It may be a flat percentage of the sales price or may be based on a sliding scale, say 5 percent the first year, declining in steps to 0 percent in year five.

Under the controversial 12b-1 plans, the fund can charge a fee to pay for its marketing and promotion costs. A 12b-1 fee can be levied on the full value of the investment each year or on the original value of the investment. The maximum fee allowable is 0.75 percent.

All funds also charge a management fee in order to compensate the asset managers for their services. These fees range from .3 percent of the funds' assets to 2 percent or even more.

Information on fees and other expense data is available on page two of every mutual fund prospectus. Investors should always read this page before purchasing a mutual fund. Investors do not always get what they pay for. Thus, the funds that charge the highest fees do not necessarily increase in value faster than the "cheaper" funds.

What is the difference between yield and total return?

Yield is the percentage return on an investor's money in terms of current prices. For bonds, it is the annual interest per bond divided by the current market price. A bond that provides interest of $96 per year and sells for 120 ($1,200 per bond) yields 8 percent.

Total return is yield plus or minus capital gains and losses. Investors should always be primarily concerned with total return and not yield. Even if a fund has an excellent yield, its return can be terrible if its principal declines. Although junk bonds had yields of 12 to 20 percent in 1989, their total return dropped 4 percent in 1989 because of declining prices.

Investors should be wary of investments promising extraordinary yields. Ask for the prospectus to get the true picture. SEC rules require disclosure of historical total returns in the prospectus.

What is the efficient market hypothesis (EMH)?

Although the EMH has been a topic of academic interest and debate for the past 25 years, it has only recently received the attention of the financial press. Market efficiency is a description of how prices in competitive markets react to new information. An efficient market is one in which prices adjust rapidly to new information and in which current prices fully reflect all available information.

The adjustments in stock or bond prices occur so rapidly that an investor cannot use publicly available information to earn above-average profits.

Although many analysts are dubious about the EMH, it does provide some important lessons that should be absorbed by all investors:

1. Tips are almost always of no value. The market processes new information very quickly.
2. A portfolio should not be churned. A strategy that involves frequent purchases and sales of securities is likely to be a loser because the commission costs eat up any profits an investor might make.
3. It is not easy to beat the market. Only a small minority of investors can consistently outperform the market. High returns can usually be achieved only through assuming greater risk. However, greater risk raises the possibility of increased losses as well as gains.

What is the difference between a primary market for securities and a secondary market?

The sale of new securities to raise funds is a primary market transaction. The proceeds of the sale of these securities represent new capital for the firm. New issues are typically underwritten by investment bankers who acquire the total issue from the company. The bankers then resell these securities in smaller units to individual and institutional investors.

After a new issue of securities is sold in the primary market, subsequent trades of the security take place in the secondary market. The secondary market is vital because it provides liquidity to investors who acquire securities in the primary market.

What is the major reason for the existence of regional stock exchanges? How do they differ from national stock exchanges?

Regional stock exchanges trade the securities of local companies that are not large enough to qualify for listing on one of the national exchanges. As a result, the listing requirements are not as stringent as those of the New York Stock Exchange or the American Stock Exchange. In addition, regional exchanges list firms that are listed on one of the national exchanges for brokers who are not members of a national exchange. This dual listing permits local brokerage firms that are not members of the New York Stock Exchange to trade shares of dual-listed stock using their membership on a regional exchange. Membership on a regional exchange is usually much less expensive than on the national exchanges.

What is the relationship between NASDAQ and the over-the-counter (OTC) market?

The OTC market is the largest segment of the secondary market in terms of the number of securities (nearly 30,000). Although OTC stocks represent many small and unseasoned companies, the range of securities traded is very wide. This market is a negotiated market where investors directly negotiate purchases and sales through dealers.

The NASDAQ system is a computerized system providing current bid and asked prices on over 5,600 of the most widely traded OTC securities. Through a dealer, a broker can instantly discover the bid and asked quotations offered by all dealers making a market in a stock. The broker can then contact the dealer offering the best price and negotiate a trade directly.

Are there any drawbacks to following the Dow Jones Industrial Average (DJIA) as a measure of market performance? Are there other stock market indicators?

The DJIA is the most widely followed barometer of stock price movements. However, the index is made up of only 30 large blue-chip companies. In addition, the DJIA is price weighted, meaning that the component stock prices are added together and the result is divided by another figure, the divisor. As a result, a high-priced stock has a greater effect on the index than a low-priced stock. A significant fluctuation in the price of one or several of the stocks in the index can distort the average.

After the DJIA, Standard & Poor's (S&P) 500-stock Index is the most widely followed stock index. On a daily basis, its movement is more representative of the movement of the stock market as a whole than the DJIA because of its larger sample size and the fact that the index is market weighted. In a market-weighted average, both the price and number of shares outstanding enter into the computation.

Why should an investor hold a diversified portfolio? What is the simplest way to diversify?

Diversification can substantially reduce the risk associated with investments. Diversification can be stated simply as not putting all your eggs in one basket. An effectively diversified portfolio reduces risk without cutting long-run average return. In selecting stocks, then, investors should be careful to choose stocks whose risks are related to different economic, political, and social factors.

A diversified portfolio is very difficult to achieve when funds are limited. For those investors with limited funds, a mutual fund offers the opportunity to participate in an investment pool that can contain hundreds of different securities.

What is growth stock?

A growth stock is defined as a company whose earnings have significantly outstripped the earnings of other companies in the past and are expected to do so in the future. These companies tend to reinvest a large part of their earnings and thus pay a relatively low dividend (or none) to shareholders. Investors who purchase these shares are more concerned with the appreciation in the market price of the stock than they are with the receipt of cash dividends.

Since these stocks provide little income, they are dependent upon high growth rates to sustain a high stock price. If these growth rates do not materialize, the stock can fall drastically. Investors in growth stocks should be aware of the greater risks associated with the possibility of earning the superior returns.

What is the difference between a bull market and a bear market? What are the implications of each to the investor?

A bull market is a prolonged rise in the price of stocks; a bear market is a prolonged decline in the price of stocks. Stock market movements are extremely important to investors. Historical studies indicate that 60 percent of stock price movements are directly related to movements in the overall market; 30 to 35 percent are related to sector or group movements, and only 5 percent are related to individual stock movements.

Because stock prices have generally risen over time, bull markets predominate over bear markets. In fact the market typically rises two out of every three years. Although bear markets tend to be of substantially shorter duration than bull markets, the decline can be steep. Even excluding the crash of 1929–32, when stock prices plunged 89 percent, the average bear market loss is about 36 percent from peak to trough.

What is the difference between an open-end and closed-end fund?

Two basic types of funds exist: closed-end funds and open-end funds. A closed-end fund is an investment company with a fixed number of shares that trades on an exchange or over the counter. Like common stock, the price of these funds changes as demand for the shares changes. Many of these stock funds trade at a discount from their net asset value.

Open-end mutual funds, by far the most popular type of fund, issue or redeem shares at the net asset value of the portfolio. Unlike closed-end funds, the number of shares is not fixed but increases as investors purchase more shares. These shares are not traded on any market and are always worth total assets minus total liabilities, divided by the number of shares.

How important is the asset allocation decision?

The asset allocation decision—how you split your dollars among stocks, bonds, cash, real estate, etc.—may be your most important investment decision. Its significance was reaffirmed in a paper published in the May–June 1991 issue of *Financial Analysts Journal* written by Brinson, Singer, and Beebower. The authors assessed the performance of 82 large pension funds over a ten-year period. Their research shows that asset allocation determines more than 90 percent of the total return. The individual stocks and other assets that the pension funds picked did little on average to improve performance over the ten-year period.

Most investors tend to pay little or no attention to how they allocate their assets. All too often, they own a hodgepodge of mutual funds or common stocks bought at various times without consideration of how they complement each other. That is a big mistake. Proper attention to asset allocation can enable you to substantially enhance your return with little or no increase in risk.

Stocks offer the best chance for investors to stay ahead of inflation over the long run. Yet, many investors continue to have as the major portion of their financial assets savings accounts, CDs, and money market deposit accounts. These investments, historically, have generated unappealing returns, particularly when adjusted for inflation and taxes.

Conservative investors should deploy at least one-third of their investment portfolio to stocks (or stock funds). A fixed amount should be set aside each month to build up the portfolio. Don't be sidetracked by gloomy predictions about the state of the economy in the financial press. Our economy will grow, corporate earnings will increase, and stock prices, in the long run, will reflect the trend in corporate earnings.

What is laddering?

Building a ladder means buying bonds or CDs scheduled to come due at several different dates in the future, rather than all in the same year. For example, an investor might buy similar amounts of bonds that mature in one year, two years, three years, and so on up to ten years. This strategy is a low-risk approach that many successful investors use.

When short-term rates are significantly lower than longer-term rates, a well-built bond ladder is likely to produce significantly higher returns than money-market funds or bank accounts.

Laddering won't produce as much income currently as buying only the highest-yielding, long-term bonds. But it is a lower-risk strategy because it entails diversification.

For example, a spike-up in interest rates would drive down prices of long-term bonds, producing losses for investors who need to sell before the bonds come due. But with a bond ladder, if rates surge, the investor will have new money to invest as bonds mature. On the other hand, a bond ladder also provides some protection if rates fall, because the investor has locked up some yields for longer periods.

The minimum amount for an effective ladder is about $50,000. Assembling a well-built ladder requires some care. Choose only high-quality bonds. U.S. Treasury bonds are among the most popular choice for bond ladders because they are backed by the full faith and credit of the U.S. government. Also, the interest income is exempt from all state and local income taxes. For investors who need more income, consider U.S. government agency issues, which are nearly as safe as Treasuries, or top-rated corporate bonds.

What is a good source of continuing information on mutual funds?

Morningstar Mutual Funds (800-876-5005) is an excellent source of information on mutual funds. It gives comprehensive fund coverage and currently tracks more than

1,500 mutual funds—both load and no-load, equity and fixed income (including municipal bond funds). It does for mutual funds what the *Value Line Investment Survey* (800-833-0046) does for common stocks.

Each mutual fund has its own one-page summary, which is updated periodically. This summary includes information such as current happenings, rankings against other funds, top holdings and how they've changed recently, the funds's performance vs. the S&P 500, and a recommendation.

Morningstar's system (from one to five stars) incorporates both return and risk. In addition, this is one of the few sources that describes the portfolio strategy of each mutual fund manager and discloses how long the manager has been in charge of the fund.

This service is expensive ($395 annually). If you're interested, you can sample it for three months ($55). Fortunately, many public libraries carry the service, so check there first.

GLOSSARY

Annuity   form of contract sold by life insurance companies that guarantees a fixed or variable payment to the buyer at some future time.

Asked or offering price   price at which a mutual fund can be purchased.

Asset   something of value owned by a firm or individual.

Basis point   one basis point equals .01 percent (or 1/100 of 1 percent)

Bear   person who believes that stock prices will drop.

Bear market   prolonged period of declining prices. These periods usually last at least several months and sometimes a year or more.

Bid or redemption price   price at which a mutual fund can be redeemed.

Bond ratings   system of evaluating the credit quality of bonds by assigning the bonds to different risk classifications.

Bull   person who believes that stock prices will rise.

Bull market   prolonged increase in the prices of securities. These markets usually last at least several months, sometimes several years.

Closed-end mutual fund   a fund that offers a fixed number of shares that are traded on exchanges like stocks and bonds.

Collateralized mortgage obligation   a debt security that is secured by high-quality mortgage-backed securities.

Common stock   fractional shares of ownership interest in a corporation.

Convertible security   a bond or share of preferred stock that can be exchanged into a specified amount of common stock at a specified price.

Corporate bond   long-term IOU of a corporation secured by specific assets or a promise to pay; generally issued in units of $1,000.

Coupon rate (stated rate)   specified rate of interest that a corporation will pay its bondholders expressed as an annual percentage of face value.

Discount rate   rate of interest charged by the Federal Reserve to member banks.

Diversification   an attempt to reduce the overall risk of a portfolio by owning different securities rather than concentrating all one's money in one or two investments.

Dollar cost average   method of accumulating money by investing a fixed amount of dollars in securities at set intervals.

Earnings per share   amount of net income attributable to each share of common stock.

Expense ratio   annual expenses divided by average net assets.

Face value (par value, maturity value)   amount the corporation must repay on the maturity date.

Federal funds rate   interest paid by banks when borrowing from other banks' reserves.

Federal Reserve System   central bank of the United States, which formulates monetary policy and controls the money supply.

Financial leverage   the accelerative effect of debt on financial returns.

Fundamental analysis   process of estimating a security's value by analyzing the basic financial and economic facts about the company that issues the security.

Ginnie Maes   securities backed by a pool of mortgages and guaranteed by the Government National Mortgage Association (GNMA).

Gross national product (GNP)   measurement of economic activity by computing the total market value of all goods and services produced in a given period.

Index funds   mutual fund with a portfolio that matches the performance of a broad-based index such as Standard & Poor's 500-stock Index.

Investment banking   the industry that specializes in assisting business firms and governments in marketing new security issues.

Junk bond   a high-risk, high-yield bond (less than BBB

rating), generally issued either by a new company or to fund a corporate takeover.

Laddering   choosing bonds or CDs with different maturity dates, and splitting your total investment more or less equally among the different bonds or CDs.

Leveraged buyout   (LBO) process of buying a corporation's stock with borrowed money, then repaying at least part of the debt from the corporation's assets.

Load fund   type of mutual fund for which the buyer must pay a sales fee, or commission, on top of the price.

Margin trading   using borrowed funds for trading.

Market efficiency   description of how prices in competitive markets react to new information.

Money market deposit account   counterpart of a money market mutual fund at a bank.

Municipal bond   tax-exempt security issued by state and local government agencies and authorities.

Mutual fund   pool of commingled funds contributed by investors and managed by a professional manager for a fee.

Net asset value per share   a fund's total assets minus its total liabilities divided by the shares outstanding.

Net worth   amount by which assets (items owned) exceed liabilities (debts).

No-load mutual fund   type of mutual fund for which no sales commission is charged to make a purchase.

NOW (negotiable order of withdrawal) accounts   interest-bearing checking accounts at a bank or savings and loan.

OTC (over-the-counter) market   trades securities through a centralized computer telephone network that links dealers across the United States.

Ponzi scheme   a scam in which the first few investors are paid interest out of the proceeds of later investors.

Preferred stock   class of stock that has certain preferential rights over common stock.

Price-earnings ratio   ratio of a share's market price to a company's earnings per share.

Primary market   the market for new issues of securities.

Prime rate   interest rate banks charge to their most creditworthy customers.

Prospectus   formal written offer to sell securities or mutual funds.

Redemption fee   charge a mutual fund levies if shares are sold before a specified date.

Secondary market   the market where securities are bought and sold subsequent to original issuance.

Securities and Exchange Commission   U.S. government agency that administers the federal laws that protect the investor.

Short sale   sale of a borrowed security with the intention of purchasing it later at a lower price.

Specialist   member of a stock exchange who is obligated to make a fair and orderly market in one or more securities.

Stock dividend   payment of a corporate dividend in the form of additional stock.

Technical analysis   process of predicting future stock price movements by analyzing the historical movement of stock prices and supply and demand forces that affect those prices.

Term insurance   form of life insurance, written for a limited period, that requires the policyholder to pay only for the cost of protection against death.

Treasury securities   debt obligations issued by the U.S. government and backed by the full faith and credit of that government.

Unit investment trust   investment vehicle that purchases a fixed portfolio of income-producing securities.

Whole life insurance   form of life insurance covering the lifetime of the insured and builds up cash value that offers protection if the insured dies.

Yield   the percentage return on an investor's money in terms of current prices.

Yield curve   graph depicting the relationship between term to maturity and yield to maturity for comparable bonds at a given time.

Yield to maturity   concept used to determine the rate of return an investor will receive if a bond is held to its maturity date.

Zero-coupon bond   a bond that does not make periodic interest payments but instead is sold at a deep discount from its face value.

INDEX